FIRST LESSONS
IN NATURE STUDY

Books by
Edith M. Patch

NATURE STUDY

Dame Bug and Her Babies

Hexapod Stories

Bird Stories

First Lessons in Nature Study

Holiday Pond

Holiday Meadow

Holiday Hill

Holiday Shore

Mountain Neighbors

Desert Neighbors

Forest Neighbors

Prairie Neighbors

NATURE AND SCIENCE READERS

Hunting

Outdoor Visits

Surprises

Through Four Seasons

Science at Home

The Work of Scientists

FIRST LESSONS
IN NATURE STUDY

by

Edith M. Patch

illustrated by

Robert J. Sim

YESTERDAY'S CLASSICS

ITHACA, NEW YORK

ISBN: 978-1-63334-099-2

Yesterday's Classics, LLC
PO Box 339
Ithaca, NY 14851

TO

ANNA BOTSFORD COMSTOCK

A WORD TO THE READER OF THIS BOOK

THIS is a book about plants and animals. Some of these plants and animals live in the city, some in the country, and some live in both places. Some of them live in the north, some in the south, some in the east, some in the west, and some in all four parts of North America.

So you see that, wherever your own home is, you are likely to meet some of the very same plants and animals that are mentioned in this book. It will not matter, however, if you meet different ones instead of the same, since different ones are just as interesting.

If you watch them when you meet them, you will see much besides what this book tells you. Perhaps, then, you will know the use of this book. It is partly to tell you interesting facts about plants and animals of different kinds, and it is even more to ask you to look and find out all you can for yourself.

EDITH M. PATCH

ORONO, MAINE

April, 1926.

CONTENTS

CHAPTER I

SUGAR

As you nibble candy and feel pleased with the taste of it, do you sometimes wonder where all the sugar in the world comes from?

BEET SUGAR

Some of it comes from beet plants. The pretty, red, tender beets we eat at the table have sugar in them, as we can tell by the sweet taste. But these red beets are not the kind that people grow for sugar. *Sugar beets* are larger and they have pale roots.

Once upon a time, about one hundred years ago, there were no fields of sugar beets growing in the United States. There were not even any seeds of sugar beets here. Then people began to bring the seeds across the ocean from France and other places where these plants grew.

At one time or another during the hundred years since the seeds were brought here for the first time, people have tried growing sugar beets in Michigan and in California and in many states between. In some of these places there are now great fields of sugar beets every year, but in some places the people would rather grow other crops. Perhaps you know whether you live in a sugar-beet state.

A field of sugar beets. The man has pulled up one of the beets and is holding it to show its thick root. The roots are sent to the sugar factory. The leaves are fed to sheep or cattle.

A beet plant puts most of its sugar into its root; so the root is the part that is sent to the factory. Sheep and cattle like to eat beet leaves, and the men who have beet fields often keep these animals so that the leaves will not be wasted. Sheep and cattle also like to eat the pulp that is left from the root after the sugar is taken out. Sometimes this pulp is given to cattle wet, just as it comes from the factory. Sometimes it is dried into a kind of beet hay. Sometimes it is kept in a silo and not used until winter.

Cattle are often kept near beet-sugar factories and are fed what is left of the roots after the sugar has been taken out.

There are many sugar-beet factories in the United States now, but there was a time when there was not one in this country or in any other country either. The French people were the first who made much sugar from beets. That was in the days when a man named Napoleon was living in France. Napoleon started some schools where people learned about sugar beets; and he told the French farmers to plant beets so that they could have that kind of sugar at home instead of needing to buy *cane sugar* from other countries.

Cane Sugar and Sorgo

Cane sugar is the kind that people in the United States used before beet sugar could be had here. Now we use both kinds.

The *sugar cane* is a plant that grows tall and straight, something like a giant corn stalk. (*Cane is a word that is sometimes used instead of stalk.*) There is sugar in a

Children who live where sugar cane grows like to bite a stalk and suck the juice.

corn plant, too, as you can tell by cutting the stalk and sucking it. And there is so much sugar in some corn seeds that we call them "sweet corn" and like to nibble them from the cob when they are cooked. But there is a great deal more sugar in the sugar cane. This plant will not grow so far north as the sugar beet will, but in the south there are cane fields so big that men have built railroads through them. When the cane is cut, it is put into the cars that are waiting on the tracks and taken at once to the mills where the juice is pressed out. There are such fields in Louisiana, where more sugar cane is grown than in any other state.

When men plant sugar cane, they do not use seeds as they do when they plant beets. They cut the stalks into pieces and put these pieces into the ground. There are buds at the places in the stalks near where the leaves drop off, and after the pieces of stalk have been in the ground for a while these buds sprout and grow up into new sugar-cane plants.

Perhaps some day you will ask your teacher to tell you about the hard times the people in Louisiana had trying to grow other crops before they began to grow sugar cane. For though sugar cane has been grown in this country a great many years longer than sugar beets, there was a time when not even sugar cane grew here.

Sorgo plants have sweet juice which people make into syrup. This picture shows how much higher than a man sorgo grows.

If you never saw a field of sugar cane, perhaps you have seen a field of *sorgo*. (This word is also written

5

sorghum.) Sorgo is grown in forty-eight states, so you would not need to travel many miles to see how it looks. It belongs in the same family of plants as sugar cane and corn. The juice is pressed out as the juice of sugar cane is. This juice is not made into sugar, but is sold as syrup.

Once there was no sorgo in this country either. No sugar beet! No sugar cane! No sorgo! What did the people do then, when they wanted something sweet to eat?

MAPLE SUGAR

In those days they used *maple sugar*. When the white men first came to America, the Indians sold them sugar made from maple trees. Then the white men learned how to make it for themselves, and they have been making it every year since. Holes are cut through the bark of the trees in the spring before the leaves grow, when the sap runs fast. Some of the sap runs out of these holes and is caught in pails. It is then poured into big kettles and boiled, getting thicker and thicker all the time until first it is syrup and then, if it is boiled a much longer time, it is sugar.

Boys and girls who visit sugar camps in Vermont or other places like to see the sugar maples because they are large and handsome trees. There is something else they like to see and like to smell and like to taste. They like to see the sap running through the holes in the bark into the pails, and they are surprised to find how much comes out through one hole. They like to drink some of the sap just as it comes from the tree to see how sweet it is before it has been boiled at all. Some of them think that the very best candy in the world is the kind that can be made by pouring thick, hot maple syrup into some snow that is packed hard in a pan. This candy is called *maple wax*. Of course you do not have to visit a sugar camp to eat maple wax. Anybody who lives where there is clean snow can make this kind of candsy, if he can get a little maple syrup to boil.

When a hole is cut through the bark of a maple tree, the sap runs out. A pail is placed to catch the sap.

Maple sugar used to be the only kind of sugar that was sold in stores in America. But now the kinds made from cane and beet plants are what we commonly buy, and some people have never tasted maple sugar.

BEES AND HONEY

The beet plant stores its sugar in its root, the sugar cane and sorgo keep their syrup in their stalks, and the maple tree has sweet sap under its bark; but many plants put their very sweetest juices into their flowers. This sweet liquid is called *nectar*.

It is from flower-cups with nectar in them that the *honeybees* sip. Honeybees made honey for themselves long before men learned how to get sugar or syrup from plants. When men found how good honey is to eat, they began to take it away from the bees. At first bees lived in hollow trees and in caves, and it was not easy for men to scoop the honey out from such places. The bees were angry when disturbed and robbed, and they fought the men.

A bee fights by using her sting. The bee's sting is like a fine, sharp needle. If she is not touched or frightened, she keeps it hidden at the tip of her body; but she can push it out very quickly when she needs to protect herself or her home.

After a while men thought of a way to get honey without frightening the bees. They made boxes which the bees could use, instead of caves or hollows in trees, for homes. Such boxes are called *beehives*. Nowadays men make hives in such a way that they can open them at the top and take out honey without being stung. Of course they must not take out all the honey, because the bees need some for themselves.

Indeed so many hundreds of bees live together in one hive that they need a great deal of honey to use for food. That is why they are so very busy all summer taking nectar from flowers and making it into honey. The bees that do this and the other work about the hives are called *workers*.

A honeybee which gathers sweet juice from flowers and makes honey of it.

A bee has a long tongue and she can poke the tip of it into a flower-cup far enough to reach the nectar at the bottom. She draws up the sweet liquid into her mouth, and from there it passes into a place inside her body that is sometimes called a *honey sac*, where it is changed into thin honey. After a worker has come home to her hive, she puts the thin honey from her honey sac into a waxen *cell* in the *honeycomb*, where it stays open to the air until it "ripens." When honey is ripe, it is thicker than when it is first put into the cell.

There are, as I have said, many hundreds of bees living together in one hive and most of them are workers. When wax is needed for the cells of the honeycomb, some of the workers make it. First they eat as much honey as they can swallow and then they hang themselves up in the hive in a sort of bee curtain. To do this each bee reaches up with her front feet and catches hold of the hind feet of the bee above her. After a while the wax forms in little flakes in some *wax pockets* which are on the under side of the bees' bodies. The workers chew this wax until it is soft and then make cells of the honeycombs with it. They use their jaws as tools when they are building the cells. The cells have six sides like little six-sided boxes, and, when the honey in them has ripened, the bees close the ends by covering them over with waxen caps.

You must not think that all the cells in a beehive are filled with honey. Many of them have baby bees in them. Such cells are called *brood cells*. Baby bees do not look like grown bees. They are fat, white, wingless, footless little things; and each one stays in its own cell. These baby bees are tended by some of the workers, which draw up partly digested food from their own stomachs and give it to the young ones.

Bees do not eat honey alone. They need *pollen*, too. Pollen is the yellow or brown "dust" that is in flowers. Worker bees gather pollen by poking it into the little hollow *pollen baskets* on their hind legs. Each worker has two of them, one on each hind leg. After the bees have brought the pollen to the hive they take it out of their baskets and pack it into cells. It is then called *beebread.* The workers eat honey and beebread for their own food and share what they eat with the baby bees.

When a baby bee is large enough to fill a cell, it is time for it to change into a grown-up brown bee with wings and legs. Such a change as this cannot be made suddenly. So the cell with the baby in it is closed over; and the young one takes a sort of nap, during which something wonderful happens in its body. When it wakens, it is a grown bee like the others in the hive; so it comes out of its cell and lives the same sort of life the other grown bees do.

There is room in this chapter to tell only a few of the things that are done by honeybees. Because so many things happen in a hive, honey is, perhaps, the most interesting sweet food we have.

APHIDS AND HONEYDEW

The tongues of honeybees are shaped for licking and sipping, and no harm comes to plants from the visits of these insects. There are some much smaller insects, however, called *aphids*, that punch holes in plants with their beaks. Through these holes they stick their long, slender mouthparts and drink as much plant juice as they need. You may not have heard as much about aphids as you have about honeybees; but there are a great many more of them in the world. There are so many kinds of aphids, indeed, that I think you cannot be among plants very much without seeing some of them.

The smallest kinds of aphids are so little that it

would take more than twenty of them going single file to make a procession an inch long. Twenty aphids of the largest kinds would make a procession about four inches long. You can take a ruler and make marks on a paper to show how long a small kind of aphid is and how long a large kind is.

You will probably be able to find some of these insects if you watch. It does not matter very much where you are when you look, for there may be aphids on the trees and bushes and other plants in a city park as well as in country places. Nearly every kind of plant that you can think of, beets and sugar cane and maple trees and roses and lilies and ferns and evergreen trees and all the rest, sometimes have aphids on them.

Many kinds of aphids are green. Some other kinds are brown or gray or pink or black or white. Whatever color they are, they are thirsty from the very first day of their lives. They can feed themselves even when they are very young. They do not need to have the older aphids feed them. Some kinds feed on the underground parts of plants. More kinds, however, spend their time on the stems or leaves or on the blossom clusters. Wherever they stay, they stick in their sharp little beaks and drink plant juice even more steadily than bees sip nectar.

Aphids suck up a great deal of juice. Some of it is used by these insects to make them grow; and some of it is passed through their bodies in clear, colorless, sweet drops. These sweet drops fall on the leaves and on the ground, and people call them *honeydew*.

Just as honey is sweeter after it has been in the

honey sac of the bee than it was when it was gathered from the flower as nectar, so honeydew is sweeter than the plant juice the aphids sip. It is a favorite drink with sweet-loving insects. Wasps come and lap it up from the leaves. Honeybees sometimes take it and mix it with their honey. And ants like it best of all.

Indeed, ants are so very fond of honeydew that they do not wait for it to be spattered around on the leaves. They creep up among the aphids and drink from the aphids' bodies. Aphids are used to this and when an ant comes up behind an aphid and touches it with its feelers, the aphid lets out a drop gently from the tip of its body. The ant laps it up before it falls. Many people have watched ants feeding among a flock of aphids; and they think it is so funny that they laugh and call the aphids the

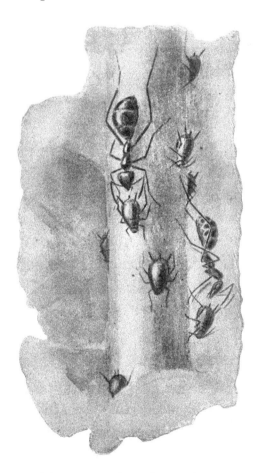

The ants taking honeydew from aphids.

"ants' cows" and say that the ants are milking their herd. Sometimes ants build a little shed over a colony of aphids on the stem of a plant. For this they use something that looks like sawdust stuck together. Sometimes ants carry their little "cows" in their mouths to fresh plants where there is a better chance to feed.

Just as maple sap changes to sugar when most of the water is boiled off in steam, and just as honey turns sugary when it is left where it dries in the sun and air, so the honeydew syrup becomes sugar when it dries.

Once I saw a whole hillside crusted over with honeydew sugar like a giant cake with sugar frosting. The sugar made a crunching sound under my shoes as I walked up the hill. There were very many evergreen trees on the hill and almost every twig was covered with aphids. The honeydew had been falling like raindrops for days, and it had dried into sugar in the sun. Indians used to gather honeydew sugar when they found a lot of it, and they ate it with their food. It has a pleasant taste.

SUGAR IN ALL GREEN PLANTS

The fact that aphids can make honeydew from so many plants shows that there is sugar in a great many more plants than beets and cane and sorgo and maple trees. Indeed, there is sugar in every growing plant that has green leaves. You do not need to visit Colorado or Louisiana or Vermont to see a sugar-making plant. You do not even need to go into the country. It is rather fun, don't you think, to know that there is sugar in grass in the park, and sugar in all the trees and bushes there? There is sugar in the growing plants in the shop window and in those at home or in the schoolroom. If you wanted to, you could put a bean or any other seed in some earth; and as soon as it grew big enough to have leaves it would begin to make sugar.

The green stuff in the leaf is what makes the sugar. It makes sugar all day while the sun shines. In the sunlight the green stuff in plants can make sugar. It cannot do this in the dark. So every plant is a sugar factory running by sunlight.

You may guess that plants would not go to all this work of making sugar all day long unless this is very important to the plant. So it is. Indeed, sugar, changed in one way or another, is the chief food the plant needs for its growth. Every plant in the world needs it.

GUESSING GAME

I know a guessing game about food that it is fun to play. The most interesting thing about this game is that if you guess back far enough you always find a green plant. It does not make one bit of difference where you start. You may begin with honey and get back to the bee and then to the flower of a green plant. You may begin with an egg and get back to the hen and then to the cracked corn the hen eats, which is the seed of a green plant. You may begin with milk and get back to the cow and then to the hay the cow eats, which is the leaves and stems of green plants. You may play this game for a day or a year; but you can never think of any real food you eat that does not lead you back to the flower or the fruit or the seed or the leaf or the stem or the root or some part of a plant that has green color.

The same thing happens if you play this guessing game about the food of any other animal besides yourself. Sometimes the hunt will be a crooked one with many turns in it; but if you do not lose your way, you will come to the green plant at last.

This is because it is only plants with green color in them that can make sugar—the substance that all animals depend upon in some way for their lives. Animals cannot make sugar for themselves; but they need it, changed in one way or another, just as much as plants do.

So when you nibble candy and feel pleased with the taste of it, there are many things for you to think about. It is interesting to know why sugar is so very, very important. It is because sugar, changed in different ways, is a food that all plants must have to keep them alive. And if there were no plants, whatever would we and all the other animals eat?

CHAPTER II

MILK AND ANIMALS THAT FEED IT TO THEIR YOUNG

You have read in the first chapter of this book that sugar, changed in one way or another, is a food that animals need.

Milk is another food that is needed by many kinds of animals. These animals need milk especially while they are babies. Indeed, it is the only sort of food that certain animals can take at all while they are very young. Animals whose babies must have milk are called *mammals*.

There are many different kinds of mammals. In this chapter you will read about some of them that are unlike in size and shape and habits. The bodies of mammals may differ from one another in many ways. But in some ways they are all alike.

Mammals all have warm red blood and breathe with lungs as birds do. But they do not have feathers. They have hair instead. Some mammals have very little hair and others are covered with thick fur.

All mammal mothers have milk to feed their babies.

They have *milk glands* in their bodies where the milk is made. The milk glands have openings where the babies can put their mouths when they suck the milk.

A human baby must have milk just as all the other little mammal babies do. If the mother is well and strong, the human baby is better off with the milk it finds in its own mother's breast than with any other kind, when it is very young.

But people learned long ago that their babies could

A goat likes to eat while it is being milked.

live on the milk of other animals, also. So people keep herds of animals for the sake of their milk. People living in the far North, where the winters are very, very cold, use the milk of reindeer. In many countries people use the milk of goats. In this country we use the milk of cows more than any other kind.

Milk is important for babies because it is the only food they can take at first. Boys and girls grow stronger if they keep on drinking milk even when they can eat other kinds of food, too. Milk is good for grown people; and it satisfies both hunger and thirst, since it is food and drink at the same time.

Soon after you drink sweet milk it *curdles*. When it curdles, it becomes thick. It curdles before you can digest it. If you drink cows' milk rapidly, as you drink water, the milk is likely to curdle in big lumps and give you a stomach ache. That is why it is a good plan to sip milk a little at a time instead of drinking it down in big mouthfuls, for then the curds will be in smaller lumps.

Goats' milk curdles in finer, softer bits than cows' milk does. People who have studied this matter say that on this account babies that are fed on goats' milk do not have colic so much as those that are given cows' milk, and that they thrive better on it.

Some people like to curdle milk before they eat it. There are different ways of doing this. One way is to squeeze lemon juice into sweet warm milk. When the milk begins to thicken, it can be stirred with a spoon or with an egg beater. If a little sugar is added, it makes a very good kind of milk lemonade.

Another way to curdle milk is to buy buttermilk tablets and put one into a pitcher of milk. The pitcher should be kept in a warm place until the milk thickens. Many people like milk this way. The tablet has *bacteria* in it. Bacteria are plants so tiny that we cannot see them unless we use a microscope. (A microscope has a piece of glass shaped so that it makes small things look large.) There are many kinds of bacteria. Some kinds are very good for our health and some kinds make us ill. Both helpful and harmful bacteria will grow in milk if they have a chance. That is why it is important that the men who handle our milk supplies should take proper care of it and keep it safe to use. The bacteria in the buttermilk tablets are harmless and to use them is an easy way to thicken milk. However, good sweet milk (if it has not been heated) usually has enough of these same bacteria so that it will have a good taste if it is allowed to "sour" in a warm place.

This is a picture of slices of toast with cottage cheese between them. Cottage cheese is one of the good foods made from sour milk.

The white, thick part of curdled milk is called *curd* and the watery thin part that separates out is called *whey*. You may have heard about little Miss Muffet who sat on a tuffet, eating her curds and whey. Curd, or thick milk, is eaten more in some other countries than in the United States. It would probably be good for us to use more of it than we do. You may like to try some with brown sugar sprinkled on top and a little bit of nutmeg grated over it.

Milk is called a perfect food because it has in it all the things our bodies need to make them grow. If you watch your mother or someone else who knows how to cook, you will be interested to see that she uses sweet milk in some things and sour, curdled milk in others.

> I made a bow to our old cow
> And said, "Good morning, Red,
> I'd like some cheese and, if you please,
> Some butter for my bread."

> And one hot day I went to say,
> "You are a friendly beast;
> So give me, please, some cream to freeze;
> A quart or two, at least."

The Cow, a Mammal with Hoofs and Horns

The feet of cows are not like those of dogs, with digging nails. Their feet have hoofs, but they are not like the hoofs of horses. Do you know what the difference is?

Perhaps you will tell me that cows do not have *horns*, and then I shall have to confess that nowadays many of them do not. Farmers have a way of rubbing something on the heads of calves that prevents horns from growing. If they forget to do that, they sometimes cut the horns off the heads of the grown cows. Cows do not shed their horns, but keep them as long as they live, unless they

When the day is hot and sunny, cows enjoy resting under a shady tree.

are taken off. It is very much easier for men to take care of cows without horns. You may have heard about the cow with a crumpled horn who tossed the maiden all forlorn. It was because cows sometimes did unpleasant things with their horns that men decided to have new-fashioned hornless cows. But, for all that, horns do look very well on cows' heads. I hope that, when people put cows into zoos for city children to see, they will choose old-fashioned cows with handsome horns.

I hope, too, that you will happen to meet a cow some day while she is chewing her *cud*. If you do, you will see that she has a contented look. She will not feel pleased if you disturb her then, for she likes to be quiet while she is chewing. When she first eats her grass and hay she does not chew it much. Then, after a while, her food comes up into her mouth again and such food is called her cud. This she grinds to bits with her strong teeth.

The cow's *milk bag* is in front of her hind legs. Her calf can find it and stand up to feed when it is only a few hours old. Sometimes a hungry calf seems to be in a hurry and bunts the milk bag with its head to make the milk come faster. This bunting habit is a funny one. If you ever try to feed a calf milk from a pail, you will find that after it puts its head into the pail it will begin to bunt. Then what will happen? More likely than not you will be having a shower bath of milk. Then I think you will laugh, since it does no good to cry about spilt milk.

The Rabbit, a Hopping Mammal

Baby rabbits are not strong enough to walk when they are very young, as calves are. They are weak and blind at first and they have no warm fur on their bodies. Their mother makes a snug straw nest for them and lines it with fur which she pulls from her own body. There they can snuggle down together and be cosy and warm.

A rabbit has long hind legs and big ears.

Their mother goes away to find food when she wants some grass or fresh green leaves, but she comes back to the nest and spends much time with her babies. When they are hungry, they suck their share of milk, which makes them grow. By the time they are three weeks old they can hop about quite fast.

There are so many kinds of animals that like rabbit meat, that a rabbit needs ways of keeping safe. One way is by kicking. Sometimes a rabbit jumps over its enemy and kicks it with its strong hind legs. But a rabbit cannot fight very well, so often it runs away from danger by taking long and lively jumps until it reaches a hiding place. Nothing suits a chased rabbit better than some bushes with thorns on them; for it has a way of creeping under the prickly branches without getting hurt, and not many animals will crowd into such places after it. Sometimes a rabbit can hide when it is very near danger, by merely keeping so still that there is no motion to show where it is.

Many animals chase rabbits and try to catch them; but rabbits have a very good time for all that. They do not *stay* frightened. As soon as danger is over they busy themselves with their own pleasant doings. With their long ears they can hear sounds that are made far off. They can turn these ears in different directions to catch noises from all around them. Sometimes they stand up on their hind legs and look to see what is near. When they do this, their front paws drop down in a pretty way.

Rabbits do not stay asleep all winter. So they need to find things to eat even when the ground is covered with snow. If you go out for a walk near some woods in winter, you may find some rabbit tracks. Perhaps you can see where the rabbits have gone to nibble tender bark from some young tree, or perhaps you can follow their tracks and find where they are hiding.

> When rabbits hop, on a winter's day,
> They throw their feet in the queerest way;
> For their long hind legs reach ahead in the snow,
> And 'tis hard to tell how the rabbits go!

25

The Pig, a Rooting Mammal

Pigs often live in dirty pens, but that is not the fault of the pigs. They like clean places. A farmer once showed me the home of his pig, whose name was Curly. Curly had a covered shed with a clean bed of straw in it and she kept the straw fresh and dry. She could go out of the door in her shed into a pen where she could run about or lie down in the sun. A stream of water ran through one corner of her pen and Curly rooted with her nose in the ground near the water. When the weather was hot Curly liked to wallow in the soft mud until she was nearly covered up in it. It made her body feel comfortable on a hot day. It was not foul, bad-smelling mud, though, and the farmer told me he thought pigs always like decent places to live in if they have a chance.

Before the farmer planted his vegetables, he used to let Curly play in the garden. That was a happy time for her. She poked into the earth with her strong nose and found many things she liked. There were *white grubs* that feed on the roots of plants for a while and then turn into brown beetles called *June beetles;* and there were other root-eating insects that the farmer was glad to have Curly eat. He said that her nose was better in some ways than a plow.

In the evening when the farmer was milking his cow, Curly used to come to the doorway which opened into her pen. She would stand up on her hind legs and put her front feet on the door sill and open her mouth. Then the farmer would throw a stream of milk into her mouth, instead of into the milk pail, until he thought he could not spare any more. That farmer was a jolly man and Curly's funny way of coming to ask for milk made him laugh.

Curly had a wooden trough in her pen where she was fed waste food from the kitchen and sour milk and some grain. Vegetables and fruits that were not suitable to sell in the market were thrown into her pen and she ate a great deal and was fat.

One baby pig is rooting in the ground with its nose. The mother pig will probably lie down on the clean hay when it is time for the little ones to eat.

When Curly grew up, she had a family of nine little baby pigs. At mealtime they used to beg for milk, too. But they did not go and ask for milk from the cow. They tagged about after their mother and made squealing noises that meant "We are hungry." Then Curly would lie down on her side and give pleasant-sounding grunts that seemed to mean "Dinner is ready." It would not take those nine pigs long to line up in a row and suck their little stomachs full of milk. They were a happy sight.

In some places in the South people do not keep their pigs in pens but let them run in the woods, where they root with their noses and find underground insects. They feed on wild plants and eat acorns and other nuts that fall to the ground. Such pigs have so much exercise that they do not grow to be so fat as pigs do that are kept in pens.

The Bat, a Flying Mammal

Most kinds of birds can fly. Many kinds of insects can fly. There are some flying fishes. Among the mammals there are flying squirrels that can spread out their side-flaps and sail from a high place to a low one; but that is not really flying. The bats, though, are mammals; and they can fly wonderfully. Just at dusk it is a strange and interesting sight to see bats flying over quiet water, whirling and dipping and swooping. They get little drinks of water that way without stopping in their flight. They get their food also without stopping, for they catch night insects while they swirl about in the air. They hunt in this way twice a day, once in the evening at dusk and once in the morning before it is light.

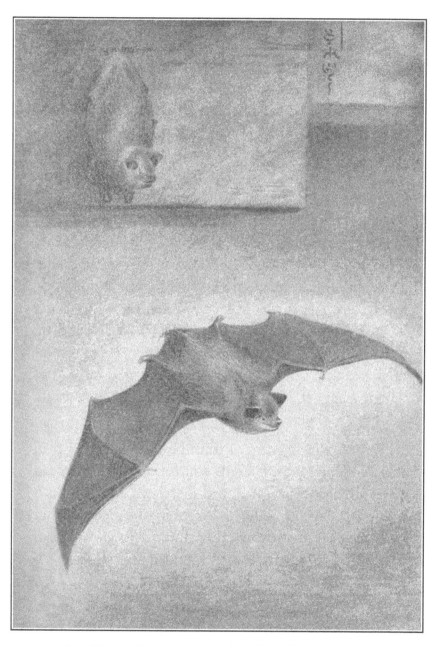

A bat flies in the morning before daylight and again in the evening. At other times it hangs itself up and rests with folded wings.

When I was a little girl, a bat came into my room one night. I saw it flying in the moonlight between my bed and the window. There was a screen in the window and the bat could not get out. It flew very near my ear, but I could not hear its wings. I lighted a lamp and hunted, but I could not find anything. After a while, when I had put out the light and was quiet, it began again its silent flight. In the morning I looked for a long time and at last found the bat. It was clinging to the wire behind a picture. I put it into a cage and tried to tame it. Its wings, when they were not stretched out, hung down limp and saggy, like a toy balloon when the air is out. There was no hair on its wings, but its body was covered with very soft fur. When I tried to touch it, the bat squeaked piteously and trembled. The little creature looked so cross and unhappy all day that at dusk I took it out of doors and let it go. So instead of having a pet bat, I watched the free ones flying near the house every evening.

When winter came, I found a bat hanging up in the woodshed. I touched its soft fur. It did not squeak or tremble or move. It stayed there stiff and still both night and day. It had been caught by the cold weather and was sleeping through the winter. This very special kind of long sleep that some kinds of animals take we call *hibernation.*

> Once there was a bat (did you know that?)
>   Who slept the winter through.
> He never saw the snow, or heard it blow.
>   A funny way to do!

30

I called the stiff little hibernating bat in the wood-shed my "pet bat"; but it disappeared when the cold weather did, so it never found out that it was a pet.

There was a man in England who once had a tame bat. When he let it flit about in his parlor, the bat would take a fly from the fingers of anyone who offered it. It would take bits of food, very carefully and gently, from the lips of its master.

Once a woman found a boy abusing a bat. She took away the trembling, frightened, little thing and kept it. After a while it would lap milk from her finger and take meat and insects from her hand. She used to let it out of doors in the evening, and it would hunt for insects for about two hours and then come back and hang itself up near the window until it was let in.

A mother bat does not make a nest for her babies. She carries them about with her as she flies. Her babies take hold of the under side of her body with their mouths and hang on so firmly that way that they do not fall. There is a fold of skin in the body of some mother bats that helps hold the young in place. When the mother finds that her young ones have grown too big and heavy to carry about in this way, she hangs them up in a safe place while she is hunting for food and then goes back to them while she rests.

Most mammals have four legs. Even the bat has bones enough for four legs. These bones, instead of being shaped to serve as legs and feet and toes, are long and slender. They spread out and make a frame for the strong, thin skin of the wings. When the wings are in use, this thin skin is spread tight like the cloth of an open umbrella. When the bat is not flying, it folds up its wings and the skin hangs close to the body.

In different countries there are different kinds and sizes of bats, with different-looking faces. In some warm countries there are big bats that eat fruit, and sometimes they eat much fruit that people want to use. In some warm countries, too, there are small bats that sometimes bite people at night if they go to sleep where it is easy for the bats to get at them. But this is such a gentle little bite that it does not hurt enough even to waken the sleeper, and the spot that is bitten heals very quickly.

All the bats in this country are very useful to us, because they eat troublesome insects such as mosquitoes that bite us, and certain beetles that damage our growing plants. The bats in this country do no harm whatever and they do much good.

People used to be silly about bats and sometimes fear them. Now that we understand their habits, we know better than to be frightened by these most interesting flying mammals.

THE WHALE, A SWIMMING MAMMAL, AND THE BIGGEST ONE OF ALL

Did you once think that a whale must be some kind of fish? Other people thought that, too, once upon a time. That was before they understood that a creature shaped so much like a fish can be a mammal and give milk to its young. The whale certainly has a fishy look. It has no hind legs at all that can be seen outside its body. Inside, however, there are a few bones that are really feeble stubs of hind legs. The front legs of the whale are paddle-shaped and are called *flippers*.

The whale's baby is sometimes called a *pup* and sometimes a *calf*. The mother whale is careful of her calf while it is very young, and stays where the water is shallow and warm. She can more easily take care of her baby in shallow water. The young calf is comfortable where the water is warm. It has a good time playing there. When it is old enough it goes on long journeys in deep water with its mother. The calf has more hair on its body than the old whales, which have only a little near their mouths.

Different kinds of whales live in different places. The most enormous kind of all lives in the Pacific Ocean. It is said that a whale of this kind can grow to be more than ninety feet in length. You can count off that number of feet on the ground with your ruler, if you want to see how long a whale can be.

Although this great whale needs much food, it does not eat big things. It goes through the water with its mouth open when it is hunting, and gathers in a lot of little sea animals and, of course, a whole mouthful of water. It keeps the tiny fishes and other small creatures it gets into its mouth, and it strains out the water with its *whalebones*, or *baleen*, which hang down in a thick fringe from its upper jaw and serve as a sieve. This kind of whale has no teeth.

All kinds of whales have fish-shaped bodies and swim in the sea.

The calf of this largest kind of whale is said to be about nineteen feet long when it is born. You can take a foot ruler and measure to see how long that would be.

There are different kinds of whales that have whalebone, or baleen, hanging in fringes from the upper part of their mouths. Besides these, there are kinds that do not have baleen in their mouths but do have teeth. The names of some kinds of toothed whales are *sperm whale*, *porpoise*, and *dolphin*. The very smallest kinds of toothed whales are only a few feet long when they are full grown.

All kinds of whales, whether young or old, whether toothed or with baleen, have fish-shaped bodies and swim in the sea. Of course there are plenty of mammals besides whales that can swim. Perhaps you can swim, yourself! There are some mammals, such as seals and beavers, that spend a great deal of time in the water. But there are no other mammals whose bodies are so fish-like that they need to live in the water all their lives.

SOME MAMMALS AT THE CIRCUS
OR THE ZOO

When you go to a circus or a zoo, you can see many interesting animals, some of which have been taken from wild places in the United States and some of which come from other countries.

The Zebra

Wild zebras live in herds in Africa. They are related to horses and have about the same shape. When you next look at a zebra, be sure to see how many things about its head and tail and feet are like those of a horse. Horses, too, were wild once, before men learned to tame and use them. There are wild horses still in a desert in Asia, and they have long, shaggy hair.

In what ways are these zebras like a horse and its colt? How are they different?

Zebras have stripes on their bodies. Some people who have seen these animals in their own wild places say that the stripes look like streaks of light and shade. Because of this zebras are hard to see when they are a little way off, and the stripes thus help them to hide.

Tigers and Lions and Panthers

The home of tigers is in Asia. The big lions come from Africa. Panthers live wild in America; once there were many more of them than there are now. These three kinds of animals, and others that have bodies shaped like theirs, are relatives of cats. Like cats, they have "whiskers" on their faces, and they have soft padded paws and sharp curved claws that can be pushed out and drawn in. When they are free, they are all hunters, as cats are.

When you see a tiger at the zoo, notice in what ways it looks like a cat.

Elephants

There are no animals anything like elephants living wild in America. There were once though, as we know, because bones of such animals have been found buried in different parts of the United States. Perhaps the next time you feed peanuts to a gentle, tame circus elephant you may think you would rather meet him there than see a wild one in the woods.

This elephant is lifting its great foot to help the driver climb to its back.

Most of the elephants seen in circuses are from India, where there are wild elephants. In India these animals are caught and tamed and taught to work. In

Africa there are elephants which are even bigger than those in India. The largest elephant ever brought to America was from Africa and his name was Jumbo.

An elephant has such a long nose that he can reach down to the ground with it without kneeling. He can reach his nose up into the branches of a tree without climbing. It is such a strong nose that he can lift heavy logs with it, and the tip of it is shaped so that he can handle small things very gently. This wonderful sort of nose is called a *trunk*.

Deer

A young calf that is frisking about the farmyard looks like a young deer in some ways. It has similar hoofs and its head is shaped much the same, but a calf is not so graceful as a young deer.

The deer are related to cattle and they have the same habit of chewing their cud. The father deer have horns, but they are different from those of cattle, for they are larger and branched. One wonderful thing about deer horns is that they drop off every year and then new ones grow again.

There are wild deer in America and in some other countries, too. It is a lovely sight to see wild deer in the woods. But these creatures are so very timid that it is much easier to see them at the zoo.

The Black Bear

There are different kinds of wild bears in America. The smallest of them are called the *black bears*. They make very lovable pets while they are young and they are fond of their human friends. When they are older they are not safe to have loose because they grow to be rough and very strong. The wild ones have very good times in the summer eating berries. Sometimes their tracks can be seen among blueberry bushes, and then people know that a bear is near.

A bear living in Yellowstone National Park.

By the time winter comes bears are fat from eating so many berries and other good things. They are, indeed, so very fat that they can live all winter without eating anything more.

Before the snow comes the black bear carries dry leaves into a deep hole in the ground or other cave.

After she has her bedroom made comfortable enough to suit her, she settles down and keeps quiet and snug and warm until spring comes. She is not too sleepy, however, to take care of her little baby bear. It is a very little baby for so big a mother to have, for a young baby bear is not much bigger than a kitten. The mother has milk enough so that the little one does not need to go without food. When spring comes the young bear has grown from a tiny, feeble, blind thing to an active little bear that can run about and climb trees and have a happy time playing.

> Once there was a bear; and she knew where,
>> If cold days came, to hide.
> She went to her den, and she didn't care when
>> Everything froze outside.

In other places in this book, you will find something about several other mammals. It is well to remember that mammals differ from all other animals in certain ways. They all have warm red blood as birds have, but they do not have feathers. They all have at least some hair on their bodies, though the hippopotamus has so little that we might as well call him "bald" all over. Most mammals have four legs, and then we call them *quadrupeds*. There are some exceptions, as you have seen, to the four-footed plan, since the bodies of some (as the bats) are fitted for flying and the bodies of some (as the whales) are fitted for swimming. People are exceptions, too, for they walk on "all fours" only when they are very young and have to creep. In one way, though, mammals are all alike—the mothers all have milk to feed to their young.

CHAPTER III

SEEDS

Suppose you had a dinner of these things:

Bean Soup

Meat Loaf   Boiled Rice

Corn-on-the-Cob

Green Peas

Sliced Tomatoes

Wheat Bread or Cornmeal Muffins

Ice Cream with Grated Nuts

Make a list of the different kinds of seeds in such a meal. If you need help in making the list, you may ask for it. Did you eat any seed-food this morning for breakfast? If you do not know, tell some older person what you ate and find out whether it had seeds in it.

Do you know what seeds a mouse or rat or squirrel will eat?

Does the farmer feed seeds to his cow and horse and pig?

What are some of the seeds that a canary or a hen will eat?

What are seeds and what are they for—merely to give food to animals?

Perhaps you will not be able to answer all those questions. I think some of them may puzzle you a bit at first. If they seem hard, wait until you have read this chapter all through and then see if you can answer the questions easily.

A seed is a baby plant. In some ways it is like an egg. It is formed in the body of a plant in the seed-cell, somewhat as an egg is formed in the body of a bird or a turtle or a frog. A bird puts her eggs into a nest and keeps them warm until they hatch and then cares for her young while they need help. A turtle puts her eggs into a hole in the sand and leaves them for the sun to keep warm. A frog puts her eggs into the water, where the polliwogs can swim when they hatch out. What do plants do for their babies?

You know how some animals can travel in the air, and some in the water, and some by land. Did you know that most plants need to travel through the air or by water or over the land? Of course plants cannot move farther than they can reach while their roots hold them fast to one place. But the baby seeds are not held fast by roots, and their little bodies are formed in such ways as to give them chances for the most wonderful journeys.

SEEDS THAT FLOAT WITH FILMY SAILS

The Dandelion

Did you ever blow the white head of a *dandelion* and watch the dainty sails go floating off, each with a seed for an anchor? Your puffs of breath started the baby dandelions off on their air trip. Who knows how far and where they went? It was a trip they needed to take if they were to have a fair chance in the world. Suppose they had dropped down between the leaves of the mother dandelion! If they had sprouted there, the sun could not reach them very well, because the old dandelion plant spreads out her lower leaves like a skirt to cover as much of the ground as she needs for herself. If she cannot share this bit of ground even with her own children, she can do something better for them. She can send up her blossom stalk straight and tall into the air and she can grow seeds with sails—lovely filmy sails. So when the yellow head of the dandelion has turned white and it is touched by your breath or a gust of wind or the breeze caused by the wing of a passing bird, then the lucky little seeds are at once up and away on their journey through the air. Every year there are many dandelion seeds sailing on the breezes; and plenty of them settle to earth and cast their anchor-seeds in spots that they can claim as their own to grow in, spreading their lower leaves like skirts to keep other plants from coming too near, just as their mothers did before them.

See how the seeds are sailing away from the open milkweed pod. The seeds of dandelions and lettuce and many other plants travel in the same way.

The Milkweed

There is a plant that children like because it has so much to show them. To begin with, there are its flat, tender leaves in spring that are good to eat if they are boiled. It is fun to gather these young plants and see the juice that comes out where the stems are broken. This juice is thick and sticky and as white as milk. It is because of the color of its juice that the plant is called *milkweed.*

The leaves of the milkweed are good food, too, for certain insects that eat them raw. A caterpillar, as striped as a zebra, feeds on milkweed leaves and then after a while changes into a big reddish and black butterfly. A red beetle with black spots on its narrow body often visits the milkweed—a queer beetle that squeaks when it is touched.

The blossoms of the milkweed are pretty to look at, and they grow in clusters near the top of the plant. After the blossoms drop, a seed pod grows where they have been. Of all the interesting things about a milkweed, perhaps there is nothing better than its big seed pod packed full of flat brown seeds with their sails folded smooth. The mother plant keeps these seeds safe from wind and rain until it is time for them to go away. Then the pod opens, and

> Sailing, sailing, on a sea of summer breeze,
> Little brown boat with fluff unfurled,
> You go where'er you please.
> Sifting, drifting, out of the harbor-pod,

46

For one gay day you float away,
Then anchor in the sod.

Spread out your sails, O little craft,
And off on pleasant journeys waft!
Your cargo is a precious seed—
We bid you, for its sake, "Good speed!"
For from the treasure that you bring
A stately plant will grow next spring.

Lettuce

There are many plants the seeds of which float with filmy sails. If you do not live where you can visit a dandelion or a milkweed or find another wild plant with such seeds, perhaps you can invite a tame one to come to visit you at home or in the schoolroom.

A few pennies will buy a whole package of *lettuce* seeds. The sails of the seeds in the package may be rubbed off, but the seeds will not be harmed. If you grow lettuce plants, first you will see the leaves which are eaten for salad. When the plants are old enough they will send up blossom stalks. Then, last of all, there will be some sailing seeds that will be ready for a journey when they are ripe.

SEEDS WITH STIFF GLIDING SAILS

Maple Seeds

Is there a maple tree near your home or along the street or in a park, where you can find it? If there is, watch the seeds scatter when they are ripe. These seeds are shaped just right for knives to put on a doll's tea table. The seeds are the handles and the stiff sails make the blades of the knives. Maple seeds are heavy. If their mother plant could hold them no higher than a dandelion, they could not travel farther than a short tumble to the ground. But a maple tree is tall and its branches are high; and the strong wind takes the seeds on gliding flights, so that many of them escape altogether from the shade of the parent tree.

The seeds in the upper right-hand corner are those of a maple tree. The others are ash tree seeds.

Pine Seeds

There are different kinds of pine trees that live in different parts of the United States. They grow wild in country places; but, because people often plant them in parks, you may find them in cities, too.

The leaves of pine trees are called *needles* because of their straight, slender, pointed shape. These leaves keep their green color and they stay on the branches all winter. Since these leaves are green in winter as well as in summer, it is easy to see why pines are called *evergreen trees.*

A pine has other interesting things growing on it besides its evergreen leaves. It has *cones*, and in the cones are seeds. These seeds are not knife-shaped like those of a maple, though their sails are flat. Perhaps you can find a pine cone some day and see for yourself what sort of seeds there are inside.

Seeds That Are Shot into the Air

Not all seeds have fluffy sails like those of the milkweed or gliding sails like those of a maple. Some seeds have no sails at all. But, for all that, they are not cheated out of a going-away party.

There are common little plants called *wood sorrel* which grow wild in many shady places out of doors. They have their leaves in three parts somewhat like those of the clovers. Some wood sorrels have white and some pink and some yellow blossoms. One kind often grows as a weed in greenhouses.

One day as I was bending over the bench in a greenhouse, I brushed my hand over some wood sorrel. I felt something hit against my face and I jumped in surprise. Then I heard little pattering sounds all about me. The wood sorrel plants were shooting off their seeds! These seeds grow in rows in slender pointed pods. When the pods dry and shrink they throw out the seeds suddenly and to a much greater distance than would seem possible.

Of course wood sorrels do not need to wait for people to come and disturb them before they can shoot their seeds. A poke from a passing bird or a push from a hopping rabbit will do just as well to set them off. Indeed, when the pods are dry and ready to pop open, a little gusty breeze is all the touch they need.

The Pepper-Box Way of Scattering Seeds

Some kinds of plants grow seeds as fine as dust in roundish box-shaped pods that open at one end. If the openings were in the bottom end, the seeds would sift down in nearly one spot and be sown much too thickly for their own good. But, because the openings are in the top end, the seeds can get out only when the stems are bent over. A strong wind can tip the pods and sprinkle the seeds at a distance.

A poppy has seed pods of a pepper-box sort. Did you ever hunt for a dry poppy pod and tip it over your hand to watch the fine seeds come out?

The Tumbling Way of Sowing Seeds

Once there was a little girl who liked nothing better than running in the wind. The harder it blew the better she liked it. As she lived near a wide prairie, she had plenty of room for running. There were no other children living near, so she used to have races with the tumble weeds.

*A poppy blossom with bud at right
and "pepper-box" seed pod at left.*

In the fall, the stem of a tumble weed breaks off near the ground, and the whole plant except its roots goes rolling about in the wind. The tumble weed has many slender branches that grow in such a way as to make the plant round enough in shape to roll; and it is light enough to be blown about easily.

It is a queer sight to see these great weeds scurrying across a prairie—whole flocks of them sometimes. It was a sight that always tempted the little girl to come out and have a race. Sometimes she caught up with one of them and sometimes (oh, very often) they all rolled and blew faster, far faster, than she could run. Sometimes one would lodge against a bush and she would sit down panting beside it to catch her breath while she watched the rest of the flock roll on and on until they were out of sight. As these plants tumbled about, their seeds were scattered over the ground. That was a gay, frolicking way of sowing seeds.

Seeds That Steal Rides

So far we have been talking about seeds that get about in an independent sort of way. But there are seeds that make nuisances of themselves. They steal rides, and often do so in unpleasant ways. If you have ever played where the *burdock* grows or the *beggar-tick* thrives, you have already made the acquaintance of two kinds of seed cases that catch on to things for free rides. Perhaps they made you feel cross because of the prickly way they clung to your coat or your stockings. Perhaps you were interested to see how they did it. They do not steal rides on the clothes of people, only. They use the coat of any animal that is shaggy enough to cling to. A dog will do, or a cow, or any moving thing they can catch hold of with their sharp points, while they ride off into new places. When the animals they are on begin to feel uncomfortable, they do just what you would do—try to rub or pull off the horrid seed cases. What could be better for the seeds inside the cases than that—to be carried on a journey and then thrown on the ground?

Seeds that travel into hair of animals and clothing of people.

Seeds That Pay for Their Rides

Many seeds that take rides with animals do not need to steal their way but pay well for their journeys.

When you eat an *apple* and throw down the core out of doors, you scatter seeds which are likely to be at a distance from the tree that bore the apple. Perhaps you have carried apple seeds as far as you have burdock seeds, but you did not feel the same way about the ride the apple seeds took. The apple paid you for your trouble.

That is what the flesh of fruits seems to be for, to pay hungry creatures for carrying seeds. The white or red or blue or yellow colors of fruits make them show

A thrush swallows a choke-cherry, seed and all.

plainly. Their beauty is like an invitation that seems to say, "Here are fresh ripe fruits that may be had for the picking!" Fruit-eating birds accept this invitation, and then what happens?

Suppose a thrush comes to a *choke-cherry* tree and swallows some of the cherries and then flies away! After a while the cherry stones come back up into the mouth of the bird and he spits them out. He keeps the soft good-tasting pulp and throws away the seeds in their hard cases. That is the way many choke-cherry trees are planted.

All bright fruits are good for birds or some other animal to eat. But you must not think that the bright colors are always invitations to people. Some of the very prettiest fruits would not taste good to you, and some would poison you. It is not safe for people to eat wild fruits just because they have lovely colors. So take the kinds that you can learn are good for you and leave the others for birds and other animals that do not make mistakes.

Squirrels carry nuts and hide them. They drop some along the way, and some that they hide they do not find again. This is the way that some of the seeds from nut trees are sown.

You will understand, I think, that anything that is so well taken care of by plants as their seeds must be very important. The seeds, being baby plants, are important if the plants are to grow year after year. But it is not necessary that every single seed should grow. That would fill the earth too full of plants. So if many seeds are used as food for birds and insects and other animals, there are still enough left to grow up into plants. That is one way animals and plants have of getting along so well together—by helping each other in such important matters as food and seed-sowing.

Squirrel with seed of a chestnut tree. Squirrels eat many nuts, but some of their nuts drop to the ground, where they can grow into trees.

SOME SEEDS THAT PEOPLE EAT

Most animals that sow seeds seem to do it in a chance sort of way. But people do it on purpose. They carry seeds from place to place and even from country to country. They plant *peas* and *beans* chiefly for the sake of using the seeds. They plant nut trees, too, for their edible seeds. Many of the seeds people eat in cooked food are called *grains*. The grains all belong to the same family of plants as the *grasses* do, and they have somewhat the same way of growing.

After the white men came to America, they brought certain grains to grow in fields for the sake of the seeds. Four of those grains they brought are *wheat* and *oats* and *barley* and *rice*. Some seeds they did not need to bring, because the Indians already had some kinds growing here before the white men came.

One very important grain that the Indians grew before white men did is *maize* or *Indian corn*. (We usually call this plant corn in this country, though this word is used in other countries to mean other kinds of grain.) Maize was much prized by the Indians, who had many stories and songs about it.

AN INDIAN HYMN OF THANKS TO MOTHER CORN

I

See! The Mother Corn comes hither,
    making all hearts glad!
Making all hearts glad!
Give her thanks, she brings a blessing;
    now, behold! she is here!

II

Yonder Mother Corn is coming, coming unto us!
Coming unto us!
Peace and plenty she is bringing; now, behold!
    she is here!

Some Plants with Two Ways of Growing

Many plants can grow only from seeds. Many plants, however, can grow from seeds and also in other ways.

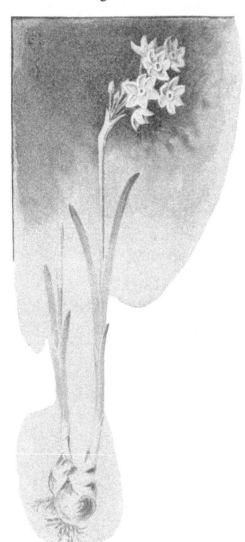

Bulbs

Plants that belong to the Lily Family can grow from seeds as other plants can. Another way lilies can grow is from *bulbs*. A bulb is a thick, somewhat ball-shaped underground part to which the roots are attached. It has layers that fit snugly together one outside another.

At first a lily plant has only one bulb, but

You may have seen a narcissus growing in a dish filled with water and little stones. Like a lily, it has a bulb.

after a while smaller bulbs form near the first one. These bulbs can be taken off and set in the ground, and will grow into lily plants that will blossom and have seeds and bulbs of their own.

Many kinds of lilies are grown only for the beauty of their blossoms. The lovely white kind called *Easter lily* is often seen in the windows of flower shops.

One very common relative of the lilies is grown for food. Did you know that when you eat an *onion* you eat the bulb of a plant that belongs to the Lily Family?

Tubers

The underground stems of some plants are thickened into parts we call *tubers*. A tuber is in one solid piece and not in layers. On the surface are *buds*, which we sometimes call *eyes*.

The tuber you know best of all is a *potato*. A potato plant can be grown from a seed, but that is not the common way of doing it. Before a farmer plants potatoes he cuts the tubers into pieces, leaving at least one bud to each piece. In this way he gets several plants from one tuber because each bud can grow into a whole plant with leaves and blossoms and tubers and roots of its own.

Another common plant with tubers is the *wild sunflower*, also called *Jerusalem artichoke*. (This last name is a very queer one for it to have, since this plant did not come from Jerusalem but lived all the time in America.) American Indians used to eat these tubers, which are good raw or boiled or roasted.

It is not unlikely that some time Jerusalem artichokes will be used for food more than they are at present. These plants can live in all parts of the United States, and a great many more bushels of their tubers can be grown on one acre of ground than of potatoes. They grow tall and have yellow blossoms. One very interesting thing about

The top of the tall stem of a wild sunflower, and two tubers which have been dug out of the ground.

these tubers is that an excellent kind of sugar can be made from them—a kind that is much sweeter than cane sugar or beet sugar. Have you ever tasted sugar made from wild sunflowers?

Slips

Did you ever see anyone start a *geranium* plant by sowing seeds? It can be done that way. Geraniums belong to the same family of plants as wood sorrels, and they have similar seed pods. But the usual way to start a new geranium is to cut off a piece of stem from an old one and put it into water. Such a piece is spoken of as a *slip.* After a slip has been in water for some time, roots begin to grow on it. Then it can be set out in earth.

A geranium plant can be grown from a "slip."

Many different kinds of plants can be started with slips. Certain trees can be grown that way. In fact, although *willow trees* have seeds, the usual way to plant them is to cut pieces from the branches of an old tree and pound them into the ground while it is soft and moist in the spring.

A large willow tree can be grown from a piece of a branch, one end of which is pushed into moist ground.

CHAPTER IV

MEAT AND HUNTERS

Plants bring into the world more seeds than there is earth for them to grow in. It is well for all living things that animals eat up the spare plants.

Animals, too, bring into the world more young than this earth has room for. If all the elephant children and grandchildren and great-grandchildren and so on lived, there would be, after a time, room for nothing but elephants; and then not room for all of them. If all the grasshopper children and grandchildren and great-grandchildren (and so on) lived, there would be, after a time, room for nothing but grasshoppers; and then not room for all of them. So, just as it is well that there are animals that eat plants for food, it is well that there are animals that eat meat for food. Animals that catch meat to eat are often called *hunters*.

HUNDRED-FOOTED HUNTERS

The word *centipede* means an animal with one hundred feet, but some kinds of centipedes have more than one hundred feet and some do not have so many. They all have long, narrow, flat bodies on the under

63

side of which are many pairs of jointed legs. If you wish to see centipedes, a good place to look is under an old board that has been lying on the ground, or under brown fallen leaves in the woods, or under the loose bark on an old log. Centipedes lurk in these dark, moist places and hunt for their food, which is chiefly such insects as they may find.

You can count the legs on one side of this centipede.

The centipedes which live in places with cold winters are small; in warmer places there are kinds that are several inches long; and in the warmest countries of all there are some that are more than twelve inches in length. Some centipedes have poison which comes out through openings in the claws on the first pair of legs. They force poison into their prey when they have caught it; and this kills their food quickly, making the mealtime easier both for the eater and the eaten.

In the United States there is one kind of centipede with only thirty legs, fifteen on each side. This kind often visits houses, where it scurries about seeking small insects that may be hiding in the house. Since most people do not like to have insects in their kitchens and other rooms, such a centipede is a very useful little house-guest.

We, who go about on two feet, find it hard to imagine what it would be like to try to travel on so many as centipedes have.

> I think it would be jolly fun
> On a hundred feet to walk or run.
> I'd race about with all my speed,
> If I had the feet of a centipede!

TEN-FOOTED HUNTERS

By a *decapod* we mean an animal with ten feet. *Crabs* and *lobsters* and *crayfishes* (or *crawfishes*) have five pairs of legs and, on this account, are called decapods.

Crayfishes

Children who wade in streams or along the banks of rivers are often afraid that crayfishes may grab their toes. I do not think a crayfish very often makes this sort of mistake; but it adds much to the excitement of wading, to expect some such adventure. I have known a child, however, to take a crayfish and bring it home and let it live in a large glass jar of water with sand in the bottom.

You may think that it would be even more fun to watch a free crayfish in the river. It would be if you could see what it is doing there; but the little fellow has a way of hiding in a hollow under a stone and blocking the door to its cave with its front claws. With so many as ten legs, the crayfish can well spare the first pair to use as arms and hands. Very good hands they make, too, as you may see if you watch a crayfish when it is eating or fighting. But do not try to shake hands with a crayfish, for its grip might hurt you.

When you find "chimneys" like these, you may know that they have been built by crayfishes.

While a crayfish hides in his cave, he sticks out his feelers and these help him to know when food is near enough to grab. At such a time an insect, a snail, a tadpole, or even another crayfish is taken and eaten. Besides such fresh meat as he kills, the crayfish will eat dead fishes if he can find them. He likes vegetable food, too, and will have salads of water-plants. If you have a pet crayfish, you can see if he will eat carrots and other plants that you like to eat; and if you ever have a chance to feed one, do not forget to look for the queer mouth-parts which help hold the food.

A crayfish does not have his skeleton inside the body and the muscles outside, the way we have. With a crayfish it is just the other way. His muscles are inside; and his skeleton is a sort of hard jointed crust on the outside. There are many good points about having a skeleton outside; but there are some difficulties. Such a firm, hard covering is not elastic enough to stretch, and it cannot grow. So every time a crayfish gets ready to change his size and be a bigger crayfish, he must get out of his skeleton to do it. A new soft, stretchy skin forms inside the skeleton, which cracks at the right time along the back. Then the crayfish can squeeze himself out and pull all his legs and his mouth parts and his eyes from their cases. Of course the new, soft, stretchy skin soon hardens and makes a new and bigger skeleton. This is a queer and wonderful way to grow.

Did you ever see how a mother crayfish takes care of her eggs and her very young babies? Did you ever hear about it? On the under side of the body a crayfish has some little fringed paddles called *swimmerets*. When the mother is ready to lay her eggs, she covers these paddles with sticky stuff that the water will not wash off. Then she glues her eggs to her paddles in little bunches. When the young hatch out, they catch hold of the swimmerets and cling there until they are able to get about by themselves.

Some of the children who read this book will perhaps be able to find crayfishes that dig little wells when the dry season comes and the water goes dry in the pond or stream. They dig until they find water, and with some of the mud they build walls around the top of the wells. These walls are called *crayfish* (or *crawfish*) *chimneys*.

A lobster (at left) and a crab (at right). Lobsters live in sea water. Crayfishes that live in fresh water look very much like small lobsters.

Crabs

Crabs are ten-footed creatures with broad, flat backs and short tails. Crabs of one kind have little curved hooks on their skeletons. They take bits of seaweed

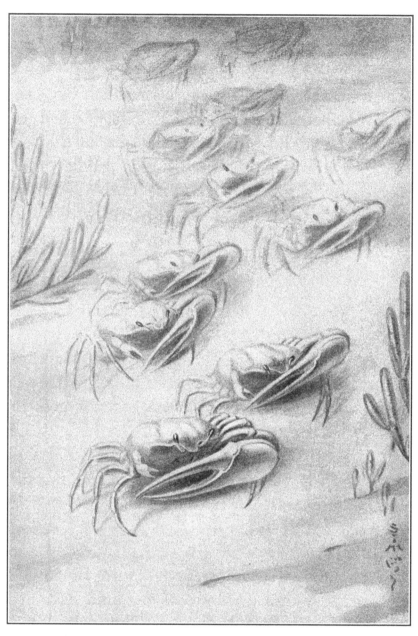

A fiddler-crab has a large claw on but one of its legs instead of on two like a lobster. It moves with a queer motion somewhat as a person's hand moves when playing a violin (fiddle).

or sponge and fasten them into the hooks, using their front claws as hands to dress themselves up in a mask. Then they can go hunting without looking like crabs; instead, they look like seaweed or sponges.

There is another kind of crab called a *hermit crab*. A hermit crab has a soft tail that might get bitten off if he did not do something about it. What he does is to twist himself, tail first, into an empty spiral shell. When he moves about he carries the shell with him. After he grows larger, he has to change to a larger shell. People who have watched him say that it is very amusing to see him slipping his tail first into one shell and then into another until he is satisfied with a well-fitting one.

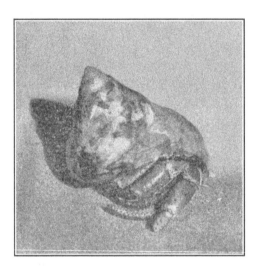

A shell with a hermit crab in it.

Eight-Footed Hunters

Daddy Longlegs

When Uncle Tom can't find his cow
At milking time, why, I know how!
I just go whistling down the wall
Where Daddy Longlegs likes to sprawl;

And while I hold one leg, I say,
"Granddaddy, tell me where to-day
Old bossy's gone"; and, first you know,
He points another foot to show.

But when I told my uncle how
To make Granddaddy find his cow,
He laughed a funny chuckling noise,
And said 'twas just a game for boys.

But it is not for cows that *Daddy Longlegs* hunts when he is left to himself. Indeed, just what he hunts does not seem to be very well understood. It would be a good plan for some of the children who read this chapter to find out more about the food habits of Daddy Longlegs or *Grandfather Graybeard*, as he is sometimes called. It would be much more interesting than holding one of his slim legs and asking him about cows. The leg usually comes off when it is handled. This would be more serious for him if he could not grow a new leg in the place of the lost one. But the new leg comes only at molting time, so it is well to touch Daddy Longlegs gently.

You may meet one of these eight-footed creatures

near your own doorstep some day at dusk when he is getting ready to creep about in the dark. Some rainy night in summer, if you open the door to your house, you may find him teetering on your doorbell. You may see him walking in a queer swinging way on the shady side of a wall. Some misty morning you may come upon him resting on a leaf near the edge of the woods.

If you watch Daddy Longlegs some day at dusk, perhaps you may learn what he finds when he hunts.

Even if you do not discover what it is he is hunting, you may have the fun of seeing him molt, if you find him when he is not yet full grown. If you thought it wonderful that a crayfish can pull his legs out of his crusty skeleton, what *would* you think to see this comical creature with his eight slim legs, as slender as hairs, coming out of their cases!

Spiders

Some of Daddy Longlegs' cousins, the *spiders*, go hunting by prowling about much as he does; but most of the spiders are stay-at-homes. Their homes are traps, but they do not catch themselves. What they do catch, you can find out by watching them and their traps. We call their traps *webs*. If you have never had the fun of watching a spider spin a web, I hope you may before another year goes by. There are so many kinds of spiders and so many kinds of webs that it would be an unlucky boy or girl who could not find at least one kind. If a spider comes to sit down beside you, do not be frightened away, like little Miss Muffet. I have always been sorry she did not stop to watch the spider. She missed such a very good time by running away.

A spider has a little drop of poison that it puts into an insect when it bites one. The poison keeps the insect from struggling. A spider does not go hunting for people as mosquitoes do, so you need not be afraid of watching one. If you do not handle it, it will not bite you. In fact it will do its best to keep out of your way.

This kind of fly spoils currants. It is well that the spider caught it.

I know a boy who once had a pet spider. He let her

make a funnel-shaped web on the window sill. When he wanted to show off his pet to his visitors, he would call, "Come, Agelena"; and out Agelena would come every time. This always surprised the visitors, for who ever heard of a spider who knew her name? The boy could have told why she came if he had wanted to. When he called, he would jiggle the web a little or drop a grain of sand on it or touch it very gently. Agelena came dashing out to see what she had caught in her web and not because she knew her name. The boy fed her flies and young grasshoppers and watched to see what she did with them.

This spider has come home from a hunting trip and is opening the door to its nest in the ground. Because of the thick flat door it spins, it is called a trap-door spider.

SIX-FOOTED HUNTERS

By *hexapods* we mean animals with six feet. The insects have six feet when they are grown up and so we call them hexapods. Like the centipedes and crayfishes and spiders, insects wear jointed outside skeletons. Insects, too, molt their skeleton-skins several times while they are growing up and changing in size and shape. A molting insect is a sight worth seeing. In fact all the strange things insects do are worth the watching. There are many kinds—more kinds of insects than there are kinds of all the other animals put together. And there is not one hexapod of the lot that does not do interesting things!

Dragon Flies

Did you ever see a dragon fly with four beautiful thin glittering wings, hunting in the air near the edge of a pond? Did he make a quick dart and catch something and then rest on the stem of a plant while he ate it? Did he use his front feet as hands to hold his food up to his strong mouth?

Dragon flies catch many mosquitoes. That is why they are called *mosquito hawks*. If it were not for dragon flies, there would be more mosquitoes to bite us. They have another name, too. Some people call them *devil's darning needles*; but that is a foolish name, because they cannot sew anything. There is a story that they can sew up the lips of children who tell lies, and the ears of

A grown-up dragon fly, which hunts in the air.

children who do not do what they are told; but that is a silly story, because they cannot harm anybody, whether good or bad. They cannot even sting, although if you catch one, it will wave its tail in a threatening way that might frighten a timid person.

Perhaps some dewy morning early, before the dragon flies are awake, you may take a walk and find one clinging to a grass stem fast asleep. If you are careful, you can pick the stem without waking the insect and take a look at it. You may wish it would waken and catch the early mosquitoes. Dragon flies do miss a great many mosquitoes by sleeping part of the time that mosquitoes are flying about.

Dragon flies do not need to wait until they are grown up before they catch mosquitoes. While they are young they live in the water, and then there is nothing they like better than tender *wrigglers*. (Wrigglers are young mosquitoes, and they swim in the water, too, until they have wings and can fly about.)

The young dragon fly does not have wings. (No insect has wings until it is grown up.) It looks different from its parent from its head to the tip of its tail. It wears a mask over its face. The mask is jointed and can move down and up the way your elbow can when you want to catch something and hold it tight against you. When the young dragon fly is near enough its prey, its mask grabs quickly, out and back again, and the wriggler or other bit of meat is held in the mask while it is being eaten.

A young dragon fly hunting in the water. It is holding its jointed "mask" away from its face. Soon it will catch the nearest young wriggler (young mosquito).

Hornets

If you see a white-faced *hornet* butting her head against the sunny side of the house or the barn, you may like to know that this is merely her way of hunting. She is bumping up against flies and not missing them any oftener than you would with a swatter. She is one of the most useful fly-swatters in the world. She catches as she swats and then she clings to something with her hind legs while she uses her front feet to help roll up her fly into a nice little sausage which she tucks under her chin. First she snips the wings off with her jaws as neatly as you could with scissors. Fly wings are not nourishing, so she throws them away.

A hornet chasing a fly.

After the hornet gets her little sausage roll all made, maybe she eats it. More likely, however, she flies off with it under her chin to her home and feeds the juicy part of it to the white squirming baby sisters that are waiting in their cells for their dinner. As there are hundreds of babies waiting, the old white-faced hunter is kept busy. She does not need to catch all the food, for her grown sisters live with her and they help, too. But they cannot all help with the hunting, as some of them have to build the paper house they live in. They have to build it bigger and bigger as the family has more and more hornets in it. Sometimes there are more than one thousand cells in the house with a baby sister growing up in every cell. It takes a great many hunters to catch

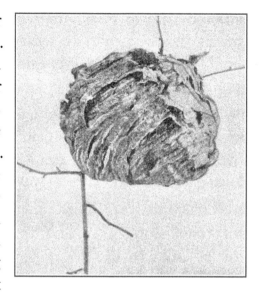

A paper nest which hornets make for a home.

flies enough for all. Since house flies grow up in very dirty places and are not clean enough to have near us, we should be thankful to hornets for catching them.

The white-faced hornet is a kind of *wasp*. There is another kind of wasp much like it, only smaller and with yellow bands on its body. This one we call the *yellow jacket*. I have sometimes heard of a boy who was stung by hornets. But if it was a boy who threw stones at a paper nest or struck a yellow jacket that came to share his picnic dinner, it served him right to get hurt. A hornet that is let alone will let people alone. It is really part of the picnic fun to let a yellow jacket have a taste of frosting or a crumb of jelly sandwich or a bit of roast chicken that it likes to tear off and fly away with.

Of course if yellow jackets come to your picnic in great numbers, it is because you are near their nest.

With too many of these hungry little uninvited guests you may not be able to eat what you want. Then you should pack your basket, very slowly, and slip away to another place as quietly as you can.

The happiest hour I ever spent with hornets was one day, when I was very small, I saw a yellow jacket fly into a currant bush. After a minute another flew down and then another. That was a sign that there was a yellow-jacket nest in the currant bush and I wanted to see it. So I lay down on the ground and crept the way I thought an Indian would do it, so quietly that there was no sound and so slowly that the weeds and grass hardly moved as I went through them. When I was near enough, I lay quite still with my elbows on the ground and my chin in my hands. Then I watched the yellow jackets building their paper nest not twelve inches from my eyes. I saw them fly down with little gray pellets under their chins. Each pellet looked like a tiny ball of clay, but it was really a wad of wet paper. They made their paper by taking bits of old wood and chewing it up in their mouths, where it became sticky with saliva. This soft little wad they spread out thin on the edge of the sheet of paper that made the outer wall of their house. They shaped the paper thin with their jaws and they helped hold it with their front feet, which they used like hands. After I had watched the yellow jackets working on their nest, I liked hornets better than ever.

I do not think, however, that it is a very good plan for us to make a practice of going quite so near a hornet nest in summer. We might sneeze! In winter we can handle such nests all we like, for then they are empty. We can even cut them open to see how they look inside.

The Fiery Hunter

The *fiery hunter* is a black beetle with shining spots on his back. If you hold him so that the light falls upon him one way, the spots look green. If you turn him so that the light touches his back from another direction, the spots look reddish like little flames.

A grown up "fiery hunter" (right) and a young one (left). Beetles like these eat caterpillars that injure our crops.

You may not like to hold him very long, for he gives off a queer smell when he is caught. I think some birds do not like that smell either, and that they let him go if they happen to catch him. The fiery hunter prowls about at night to find his food. He likes *cutworms*. (Cutworms are caterpillars that hide in the ground during the day. At night they feed by cutting off the stems of plants or by climbing up and eating blossoms or leaves. They often do much damage to crops.)

Young fiery hunters do not look at all like their handsome parents. They are flat and long and scrawny and they have no fiery spots of color on their backs. But they can hunt just as well. They hunt for themselves from the day they are hatched and do not have to be fed like baby hornets. They live under stones or pieces of wood, and they eat the same sort of food that the grown ones do, only more of it; for they need a great deal to grow on.

In this chapter, you have read about a number of kinds of hunters. Some can swim and some can creep and some can fly. They have different numbers of feet and they do not look alike; but, in some ways, they are all alike. They all have jointed bodies and jointed legs. Each hunter in this chapter has the hardest part of its body on the outside. Not one of them has a backbone.

CHAPTER V

HUNTERS THAT HAVE BACKBONES

In this chapter you will read about different kinds of hunters. Some have their homes in the water, some in trees, and some on the ground. Some have scales and some have feathers and some have hair. Some can swim and some can crawl and some can fly and some can walk. They do not look alike; but in one way they are alike. They all have backbones.

FINNY HUNTERS

Perhaps you have looked at a fish. Did you see *scales* on its body, placed somewhat like shingles on a roof? The scales are smooth, and the body of the fish can slip easily through the water.

Did you find out what parts of the fish are called *fins*? Do you think that a fish uses its fins in swimming in some of the ways that a bird uses its wings in flying? When next you look at a fish, see if you can find at least three unpaired fins, one on its back, one on its tail, and one on the lower part of its body. Besides these single fins, see if you can find two pairs of fins. One pair is higher on the sides of the body than the other pair. The fins of the higher pair grow instead of the front legs that some animals have. The fins of the lower pair grow instead of the hind legs of some animals.

If you can find a fish to watch in a brook or in a glass tank or bowl, see if it opens and shuts its mouth very often. A fish takes a great deal of water into its mouth; but this is not because it is thirsty. The water goes into its mouth and out through openings in the sides of its head. These openings are called *gill slits*, because they are near the *gills*. The water has air in it, and, as it washes over the gills, the air reaches the blood in the gills. That is the way the fish breathes. When you breathe, the air reaches the blood in your lungs. You cannot breathe with water in your lungs, and the fish cannot breathe with dry air on its gills.

Salmon, the Leaper

The old salmon live most of the time in the sea. There are different kinds of salmon that grow to different sizes. One kind, which lives in the Atlantic Ocean, is called the common Atlantic salmon. One of these salmon that weighs about twenty pounds is thought nowadays to be a big one, though years ago some of them used to grow so large that they weighed forty pounds.

The salmon have the water of the whole ocean before them, and they swim where they can find young crabs and other food that they like to eat. Some people think that they do not go very many miles away from the shore.

"If the falls are not too high, the salmon leap over them."

Before they are ready to lay their eggs, the salmon take a journey. They swim into a river and travel up the river until they find a small stream that seems to be the right place for their nest. In many rivers there are waterfalls. If the falls are not too high, the salmon leap over them. Before they lay their eggs they must find a place like the one they were in when they were eggs themselves. The right place for a salmon nest is where the water is shallow and the bed of the stream has little pebbles or gravel.

When such a place is found, a salmon plows a trough in the gravel, in which many eggs are laid. Then the fish scatters a little gravel over the first eggs before more are laid. The father salmon stays at the nesting place until the mother salmon has laid thousands of eggs. Then the old salmon leave their eggs to hatch when it is time. Salmon eggs are laid in the fall when the water is cool, and they do not hatch until spring.

At first a tiny salmon does not swim and does not eat. It is not hungry, because even after it is hatched there is still some of the egg yolk fastened to its body. As long as the yolk lasts, the little fish lies quietly among the pebbles in the water. After the yolk is all used up, the young fish is hungry and begins to swim about and hunt for bits of food.

Salt water would kill the very young salmon, and they do not leave the fresh water until they are old enough to live in the ocean.

In the Pacific Ocean, off the coast of the United States, there are five kinds of salmon. You need not try to remember their names, but perhaps you will like to hear what they are. The largest kind is the *king salmon*. Sometimes a king salmon may weigh one hundred pounds. Is that more than you weigh? The smallest kind is the *humpback salmon*, which weighs from three pounds to about ten. Besides these, there are the *blueback salmon*, the *silver salmon*, and the *dog salmon*. Each kind of salmon has several names, and perhaps you know them by other names than the ones I have used.

People like to eat the flesh of salmon, and great numbers of the fish are caught for food. Every year the first salmon that is taken in the Penobscot River in Maine is sent to the President of the United States.

There are more salmon caught in the West than in the East. One year in Alaska there were so many of these fish taken that if they had all been loaded on freight cars, it would have taken a train one hundred miles long to carry them. These western salmon are canned and sold in all parts of the country.

You may wonder that there can be any salmon left in the world when so many are caught for food. There are not so many as there were once; but people have learned how to take care of these fish while they are young, so there are a great many that go down the rivers to the sea every year. The places where the young salmon are taken care of are called *fish hatcheries*. There are many kinds of fish besides salmon that are taken care of in fish hatcheries while they are little.

Common Codfish

The codfish live in the sea all their lives. They usually grow to weigh from about twelve to about thirty-five pounds, but sometimes they are much larger. Once one was caught near the coast of New England that weighed more than two hundred pounds and was more than six feet long. Do you know a man who is six feet tall and who weighs about two hundred pounds?

Codfish swallow many queer things. Small iron tools and children's toys that happen to be dropped in the ocean are often swallowed whole by these fish, and sea shells and stones are found in their stomachs.

Many codfish are caught by men for food. Some are sold to be eaten soon after they are caught, but most of them are dried and salted so that they will keep a long time.

One codfish can lay more than a million eggs in one year. If all the eggs hatched and all the fish grew up, the sea would soon be full of codfish. These eggs rise to the top of the water and drift about. Many of them are eaten by sea animals for food, and many are washed ashore, where they cannot hatch. People like to be sure that there will be plenty of codfish, so they take care of some of the eggs until they hatch, and keep the little fish until they are old enough to swim about in the sea.

FOOTLESS HUNTERS

If you live in Minneapolis, Minnesota, it will not take you long to think of the name of a footless hunter; for boys and girls who live in that city can visit the Museum of the Public Library and get acquainted with the pet snakes there. If you live in New York City, you have perhaps visited the Reptile House in the Zoological Park. In many other cities, too, you will have a chance to watch live snakes. But you do not have to live in a city to meet a snake; for, of course, snakes run wild before they are caught and kept in museums and parks.

These harmless snakes and turtles are so kindly treated that they are not afraid of boys. Children who live in Minneapolis visit the Museum of the Public Library for the pleasure of playing with these pets.

Perhaps you have had a pet *garter snake* of your own. This is the commonest kind of snake we have in this country. A garter snake does not lay her eggs. She carries them about inside her body until they hatch. In this way she keeps the eggs safe. Her young snakes are able to crawl as soon as they are born. The little ones like to hunt for earthworms.

Some snakes have *poison fangs*. When they are hunting they press some poison into their prey when they bite it, so that it is dead or stunned while it is being eaten. That makes the meal easy for the snake and comfortable for the prey. (You may remember that there are other hunters that poison their prey.)

The daintiest snakes in the United States are the little *green snakes*. They are as green as grass, and their color makes them hard to see. They hunt for smooth caterpillars and crickets and grasshoppers. A mother green snake does not keep her eggs inside her body until they hatch, but seeks a good place and hides them there. Snakes of this kind are interesting and pretty pets.

Like all other wild animals, however, snakes are even more interesting in their own free homes than in cages. "The way of a serpent upon a rock" was one of the wonderful things that a wise man named Solomon liked to think about.

FEATHERED HUNTERS

A hunting bird has its body shaped to help it in hunting, just as are the bodies of other hunting animals. The *chickadee* has the right sort of little bill for picking up insect eggs, and the right sort of clinging feet for swinging upside down on a branch while it is seeking food. A *woodpecker* has a strong neck and a strong bill for the business of pecking out the insects that hide in

A hawk resting on a post. It flies swiftly when hunting.

90

or under the bark of trees. The *swallow*, which skims over the meadow, some days high and some days low, depending on where the insects are thickest, has long oar-like wings and a rudder-like tail which makes its flight look like swimming in the air. This bird can turn quickly when it needs to catch a very lively insect. *Hawks and eagles* have sharp gripping claws, and tearing bills, and eyes that see a little movement far away, and wings that can reach their prey swiftly.

Besides these active hunters, there are some birds that stand and wait. The *herons*, with long stilt-like legs, are patient hunters of fish. You might think, to see one, that it had gone to sleep on one slender leg. But let a fish swim close, and you will notice that the bird is awake and swift with its bill when the time comes to use it.

A heron stands still while it hunts, sometimes on one leg, sometimes on both legs.

Perhaps of all the hunters of meat, there is none more beautiful than a heron in quiet water with the slender water plants behind it. And I hope one day at dusk you will be where you can see an evergreen tree on the shore of water that is colored by the sunset skies and on the branch of the tree, a heron!

The reason why I do not say more about the feathered hunters in this chapter is that there will be birds in other pages of this book. But this is the place to say that of all the hunters in the world, none is more useful to men than an insect-eating bird. A man who protects such a bird protects his own daily bread. But if you have eyes for beauty and ears for song, you will know other reasons, too, for liking birds.

HUNTERS OF CARRION

Danny, a boy four years old who lives next door to me, said one day, wistfully, "Sandy likes clean bones, *only*." Sandy is the short name for my dog. His full name is Alexander Macgreggor McLeod, for he is a Scottish terrier and needs a Scotch name. I think Danny said "Sandy likes clean bones, only" because he *wanted* the little dog to like clean food. Everybody who loves a dog would be glad to have him like clean food, only; but in spite of our wishes, he always likes dirty food, too. Not only that, but he likes dirty food best of all. Sandy has plenty of clean food—good milk, vegetables, and cereals. He has plenty of clean bones, too; marrow bones with meat on them fresh from the market. Such a bone he accepts politely and gnaws on it while anyone is about; but as soon as he thinks no one is watching, off he goes to the plowed field or garden. The next thing we see is a little dog with his paws dirty from digging and his nose smudgy from rooting. Sandy has buried his bone! It is too fresh to please him.

To be sure, Sandy hunts live things. He will chase a squirrel until he scares it up a tree and then barks frantic dares to it to come down and be chased again. He will run a rabbit under a brush pile and dig for hours to get the rabbit out, though by the time he stops digging the rabbit is usually under another brush pile far away. He will scare a feeding bird and then stretch and jump as if trying his best to follow it up into the air. So eager, indeed, is Sandy to hunt any moving thing that while the sandpipers are nesting and before the young partridges can fly we keep the little rascal away from the river ledge and out of the woods.

Sandy is waiting for someone to come to play with him.

But all that is just for fun, because he loves to chase things. He is a frisky dog and will scamper away after windswept leaves or blowing snow. Suddenly in the midst of some frolic, he sniffs a scent that is of real importance to him. His nose will quiver and off he will go. In a little while he will come back with some bad-smelling food to eat. Then he must have a bath before he is fit to come into the house.

The dirty food that dogs like to find in garbage

heaps and such places is sometimes called *carrion*; and animals that eat carrion are called *scavengers*. There are many scavengers besides dogs in the world, and some of them are very helpful in keeping the air and the earth and the water clean and pleasant enough for people.

Of course nowadays men know how to take care of most of the garbage by burning or burying it. But a long time ago they did not understand how unsafe it is to have such stuff about; and in those days it was a good thing for men that there were wild dogs and jackals and other scavengers to help keep the dooryards clean.

Even now, men cannot keep the whole earth clean without help. There are some birds that help. *Buzzards* do their part to clean up the land in warm places, and *gulls* do their part to clean up the sea. In countries where *storks* live, they do much to eat up food that is thrown away.

A gull in the area, watching the sea.

(Some insects, too, are useful scavengers. It is not only animals with backbones that help keep the earth clean.)

You find the fields sweet-smelling and fresh. You find the air pure enough to breathe. You find water good to drink. You find the lake clean enough for your swimming. You find the seashore fit for a playground. Then never forget to be thankful that there are creatures flying in the air and swimming in the water and running on the land that do not like clean food, *only*.

Four-Footed Hunters

A quadruped, as you have learned, is an animal with four feet. There are so many quadrupeds that hunt, that you would not need to try very hard to remember some of them. Perhaps the first one you would think of would be the *cat*. You may know that one best.

Kittens are born hunters and are ready to begin while they are very small. They will play at hunting a piece of twisted paper that you drag about on a string, pouncing down on it and holding it with their claws to keep it from getting away. They will push a ball and hunt it while it rolls. They will hunt each other in a frolicking sort of game that is a delight to watch. They will hunt the wind-swayed grass in the fields, crouching and following along with light and stealthy tread, their little bodies happy in the hunt from the tip of the pointed ears to the tip of the swinging tail. Yes, they love to hunt. You cannot watch them at it and doubt their pleasure. Their bodies are shaped perfectly for hunting. Their soft padded paws, their sharp claws that can be drawn in or pushed out, their quick-hearing ears, their eyes that see by day and by night, their sharp teeth—oh, they are hunters with every bit of their beautiful bodies.

During the summer, when out of doors, Buster was tied by a very long cord to an overhead wire. He was healthy and happy and caught no birds.

Cats hunt for themselves and for their kittens. They creep quietly forth at night and watch beside a mouse hole; or they look under the barn where the rats have runways; or just before dawn, they prowl through the dewy bushes and catch a bird still asleep; or they climb a tree and empty a nest of baby robins; or, of a hot, drowsy summer afternoon, when some robins are out of their nest but not yet able to fly, they lie in wait and spring upon the young birds, who stand no chance of escape. All these things cats do; and some of these things we wish very, very much that they would not do.

A cat cannot help being a hunter, and so is no more to be blamed than a dragon fly catching mosquitoes or a hornet catching flies. The *cat* is not to be blamed for the young robin it kills, but perhaps *the person who owns the cat* is responsible for the death of the bird. That is something for you to think about. It is a question with several sides to it.

One side might be called the food side of the cat problem. There are many kinds of insects that do damage to plants of forest and field and garden. They eat the crops the farmer grows; they eat the grass he needs for his cows; they eat the grain he needs for his hens. What would any of us do without the plants the farmer raises for us to eat, without milk from his cows, and without eggs from his hens? Of all the insect-hunters, there are none more valuable than the birds. Anything that lessens the number of insect-eating birds does harm to our food supply. Birds are valuable to the farmer and therefore important to us all.

Do cats do any good to our food supply? They catch rats and mice, eaters of grain and some other food of ours. If there were no other way of getting rid of troublesome rats and mice, cats would be needed for this help. But rats and mice can be caught in traps or poisoned much more rapidly than they can be killed off by cats. So we do not really need cats to protect our food supplies.

There is another side to the cat problem that might be called the pleasure side. Many people like cats. They like to have them in their homes. Is this pleasure more important than the harm cats do? You may not be able to answer that question now, but you might begin to think about it. And while you are thinking about the pleasure that cats and kittens give people, it is only fair to think, too, about the pleasure that birds give people—by their song and beauty and their wonderful ways. There is this to think about, too—that birds were here in America first, before the white men came and brought cats. In a way, this country "belonged" to them first. Was it a good plan for white men to bring cats to America and let them kill birds? Is it a good plan for us to let stray cats roam the fields and woods and parks?

Of course it is not fair to blame the cats for being what they are born to be—hunters. They are hunters just as naturally as their big relatives, the lions and tigers, are. But when people have pet lions and tigers, they keep them in cages where they can do no harm. How should pet cats be kept? Shut up in the house every night and most of the daytime, too, during the season when birds are nesting and while there are young birds about!

Two-Footed Hunters

When Indians were the only people in North America, they hunted with bows and arrows for their meat. Nobody knows how many hundreds of years they had been doing it. They hunted in a wise way, and there was always plenty for them to find. They took what they needed for food, but they did not kill off whole herds of buffalo for fun and they did not slaughter whole flocks of passenger pigeons. When white men came, the ponds and fields and woods had game in great abundance. If white men had hunted as wisely as the Indians, there would still be a great abundance of game. The white men came less than five hundred years ago. I am not going to tell you here what became of the buffalo and the passenger pigeons and most of the other game, except to say that people have hunted in wasteful and wicked ways.

Civilized men in most places have very little need of wild birds and beasts to eat. They can eat beef cattle and sheep and hogs and hens and ducks and such other animals as they can raise. So most of the hunting that men do these days is not for need but for pleasure.

What pleasure does a man find in hunting? Perhaps you can think of many things a hunter can enjoy. He walks through woods and finds his way among the trees. He wanders along the banks of pleasant rivers. He passes fields of flowers. He hears the songs of birds. He sees, perhaps, a bear having a good time eating blueberries; or, perhaps, a little spotted fawn with its mother deer; or, perhaps, a flock of wild ducks swimming in a pond. He has plenty of healthy outdoor exercise and a relish for his food. Hunters have told me that they love all that part of life in country places; and if you like being out of doors yourself, you can understand that hunters may have very good times.

It used to be the fashion for nearly all hunters to carry guns or traps or fishing rods. Such hunters were proud if they could shoot quickly enough to kill a flying duck or a running deer. They sometimes bragged if they caught wise old bears in their traps. They often boasted about the number and size of the fish they pulled out of the stream.

There are many hunters, still, who go about in wild country places with guns and traps and fishing rods. But every year there are more and more hunters who leave those things at home, and carry, instead, cameras and notebooks. These gunless hunters can walk in all the beautiful wild places and see the birds and beasts and blossoms that live there. They bring away memories of happy, deathless hunting; and, to help their friends share the pleasure that they have had, they bring pictures of live wild animals and birds and stories about their habits.

What do you think of this way of hunting? The baby deer (fawn) seems to find it pleasant and interesting to meet a hunter like this.

No doubt many of you who read this book will some day be such hunters yourselves, having good times taking pictures of wild creatures and making notes about the interesting things they do. When that time comes you will be sorry if hunters with guns and traps have not left plenty of happy wild things in country places. You can see that it is very important that there should be the right sort of laws about hunting.

Indeed, hunting laws are such very important matters that in May, 1924, the President of the United States called a meeting of people to talk about *Outdoor Recreation*. Many of the wisest men in this country went to that meeting. Perhaps you would like to find out something about what they said. I think some member of the *Junior Audubon Clubs* will know; and as more than two million children belong to these clubs, perhaps some of your own school friends can talk with you about ways to help take care of wild things. The time will come when you will be old enough to help make laws for two-footed hunters. You will want to know what sort of laws are right both for the hunters and for the hunted things.

CHAPTER VI

THE COTTON PLANT AND SOME OF ITS RELATIVES

In another chapter of this book, you read about wheat and oats and barley and rice and other seeds that were carried from one country to another by men who wished to grow more of these seeds to use in new places. The seed of the cotton plant might have been spoken of in that chapter, if we had not saved its story to tell by itself.

The places where cotton plants grew first, before men took their seeds to other parts of the world, were all in hot countries and islands. In hot climates the cotton plants live from year to year, and some kinds grow to be large-sized shrubs and one kind is a small tree. On account of the size of these plants where they grow wild, it is quite common to speak of the "cotton tree." But when men take the seeds and plant them in places where there is frost in winter, the cotton plants die each year and never grow to be as large as they do in hot climates. In this country the seeds have to be planted every year, and these seeds grow into plants from two to seven feet high. The difference in height depends partly on the kind of cotton and partly on the kind of soil and the weather.

Cotton is grown in the southern part of this country. If you live in one of the Southern states, perhaps you can visit a cotton field and notice just how the seeds look before they are picked out of the open pods. If you do not live where you can see a cotton field for yourself, perhaps your teacher will ask someone in the South to send a seed pod with ripe seeds in it.

Two cotton plants, or "trees," with their bolls fully opened, ready to be gathered.

The seed pod of this plant is called a *cotton boll*. A full-grown large cotton boll, before it is open, is about the size and somewhat the shape of a hen's egg, with one end pointed. When the pod opens, the fine *lint* that grows on the seed is beautiful and fluffy. This fluff looks very much like the fleece that grows on a sheep. It is for this reason that some people used to call the cotton plant the "vegetable lamb."

103

There are different kinds of cotton plants. The lint (or *fiber*) on the seed of some is white. Others have yellow or reddish or brown lint. The chief kind that is grown in this country has a pearly white fiber which is sometimes less and sometimes more than an inch long. A cotton fiber has twists in it somewhat like the twists in a corkscrew. A fiber is so fine that you cannot see these twists unless you look at it through a microscope. When the lint is made into thread, the twists in one fiber catch into those of another, and this helps to make the thread strong.

If you take the cotton out of the boll, and pull the fibers away from the seeds, you can twist a coarse thread for yourself. To do this you will hold a handful of fibers in your left hand, and then with the thumb and first finger of the right hand you will take a few fibers and gently twist them together and pull them carefully. In this way a long thread can be made of these short fibers, because they catch and hold together by means of the twists in them.

People could have cotton thread even if they had no machinery with which to make it. People can weave the thread into cloth by hand, too, if they make a simple frame to hold the threads. Perhaps you have done a little weaving at school.

When Columbus first sailed to the West Indies, the people who lived on some of the islands went out to meet him in canoes and held out cotton yarn for him to see. He could tell by their motions that they wanted to trade with him, although he could not understand what they said. He found the people in Cuba using hammocks made of cotton cord.

Long before the time of Columbus, the Hopi Indians who lived in the Southwest made cotton cloth from a kind of cotton that grows in what is now called Arizona. These Indians thought so highly of the plant from which they got their clothing that it was a custom with them to use the fiber and things made from it when they prayed. Their prayer sticks were tied together with cotton string. When a Hopi girl was to be married, all the men who were friends of the bridegroom met and made her a blanket and other cotton things to wear.

Cotton can be picked, pulled from the seed, made into thread, and woven into cloth without machines; but it is slow work if done in that way and it takes a long time to make a very little cloth. People need much more cloth than there is time to make by hand, and the men who have invented machinery to use in making cotton cloth have been a great help to us. You have probably heard of one of these men, Eli Whitney, who invented a machine for pulling the fiber off the seeds. Such a machine is called a *cotton gin*.

Some day, if you go to the city of Washington, you can see in a museum there the very gin that Eli Whitney made. It is called a "saw gin" because it has a part like a circular saw, with teeth on it like saw teeth. Since that first saw gin was made, this sort of machine has been improved and enlarged until now one of them can gin as much cotton in a day as a man would be likely to gin by hand in a whole year.

Of course, as you know, machines have been invented for spinning thread and weaving cloth, so that great amounts of such work can now be done in mills and factories. If you live near a cotton mill, perhaps you can find someone who will take you to see how cloth is woven.

Machines have been invented, too, to pick the cotton in the field, but they do not work very well. So cotton is picked by hand to-day, just as it was hundreds of years ago.

It is not hard to learn how to pick cotton. It is so simple that a child can do it. It is fun to pick a little cotton, but it is hard work to keep at it a long time. One thing that makes cotton picking hard work is that there is such a tremendous lot of it. The bag a picker carries grows heavier and heavier before it is full enough to empty. It is hard, too, for the picker to stoop while he works. Another thing that makes this job a hard one is that the cotton field is so hot. Cotton must be picked while the sun is shining and the lint is dry and fluffy. The heaviness of the bag and the stooping position and the heat make the pickers so tired that some people who own cotton fields think that it is a good plan to give the pickers some pleasure mixed with the work. Something cool to drink and something to eat is sometimes kept near the baskets where the pickers empty their cotton. The pickers like to sing, too, and music helps to pass the time cheerfully.

The fluffy cotton in the ripe, open boll is not the only beautiful thing about the cotton plant. The flowers

The lower picture shows blossoms and leaves of the cotton plant. Above is an open boll.

are pretty, too. Cotton blossoms look much like white or pink or yellow or red *hollyhock* blossoms—not double hollyhocks but the single ones that have five lovely petals. There is a good reason why hollyhocks and cotton plants should have flowers that look alike,

107

for they belong to the very same family of plants. This is called the *Mallow Family.*

Perhaps you know some plant that belongs to this family. There is a very common small one that is sometimes called "shirt-button plant" and sometimes called "cheeses." It seems queer to call the same plant by two names so different. This is the reason. The parts with the seeds in them grow in circles that are about the size of shirt-buttons. These circles are made up of wedge-shaped pieces like pieces cut out of a round cheese. Another name for this plant is *common mallow.* Children like to hunt for the little cheeses and eat them.

The reason why mallow cheeses have a pleasing taste is that there is mucilage in them, for some kinds of plant mucilage are good to eat. Grown people, as well as children, like mallow mucilage and use one kind in their cooking. This kind is in the seed pod of *gumbo* or *okra.* Some okra pods grow to be more than a foot long. By that time they are too tough to use for cooking. They are best when they are green and tender and about three inches long. These young pods are used for thickening soups and stews, and they are sometimes cooked whole and served as vegetables. Sometimes the pods are left on the plants until the seeds are ripe, and then the seeds are roasted and used instead of coffee.

There is another kind of food we owe to this same family of plants. You may have guessed that it is the *marsh mallow.* The mucilage that makes this kind of candy so sticky comes from the root of a plant called

Common mallow. Find the "cheese," or "shirt-button." Notice that the flowers, though tiny, are shaped much like single hollyhocks.

marsh mallow because it is a mallow that grows in marshes.

Nor is the cotton plant behind the rest of the Mallow Family in giving us things to eat. For a long time people who raised cotton for the lint burned the seeds or threw them away. There were so many seeds that it was

Marsh mallow plant. Do the leaves and flowers resemble those of the cotton plant?

troublesome to get rid of all of them. But after a while people found out that the seeds are good to use, and now the seeds are considered to be worth about one-sixth as much as the lint itself.

The cotton seeds are a little like coffee beans in size and shape. After the hull is taken off, the kernels or meats have very good food in them. The oil in them is taken out and used for salad oil, and for making *oleomargarine* to use instead of butter to put on bread, and to use instead of lard in cooking. (Some people call this kind of food *margarine* and some call it *oleo*, because they do not like the long name.) Some of the oil is also used for making soap.

Some of the kernels, after the oil has been removed, can be ground into flour for people to use. This cottonseed flour is good to mix with other kinds in making breakfast food, biscuits, muffins, bread, cake, pie crust, and other food.

The cotton plant helps clothe us and helps feed us and helps keep us clean.

There are other animals besides people that like to eat food prepared from cottonseed. Cottonseed meal is a very important food for cows. This meal is fed not only to cattle that live in the South; it is such a good food for cows that people have brought it a long way into the North and use it there, too. Cottonseed meal is an important part of the food that is given to cows in Maine. If you look at a map, you will see that Maine is not near the "cotton belt" (that part of the country where cotton is grown). You can know by this that cottonseed meal must be very good, or men would not pay to have it brought so far.

Some animals do not wait to have parts of the cotton plant prepared and brought to them. They go into the field and help themselves. Most of the animals that do that are the six-legged ones that we call insects.

Honeybees are insects that visit the cotton flowers and take away nectar and make it into honey. Cotton honey is so light in color that it is called a "white honey," and it is a very good kind indeed. In the cotton belt, cotton honey is the chief kind that bees make. They make more than they need for themselves, and people are glad to have what honey the bees can spare.

There are more than five hundred kinds of insects that go into the cotton fields. Some kinds fly in only to visit the flowers, as bees do for the pollen and nectar they find there, and these do no harm to the cotton plant. Some stay in the cotton fields all their lives from the time they hatch out of their egg shells until they are grown up. These chew the leaves or eat the tender bolls or suck juice out of the plants; and some of them damage the cotton so greatly that they are called pests. One pest, a long-beaked beetle, is called the *boll weevil*. One, a hairless caterpillar that belongs to the same family as the cutworms, is called the *bollworm*. One, a small aphid with green or black or pale yellow colors, is called the *cotton aphid*.

Although there are a great many creatures that look to the cotton plant for a living, only Man can plant the cotton and take care of it, and pick the lint and make cloth with it.

This chapter has not told all the uses to which cotton lint is put. So you can have the fun of seeing how many things you can think of that are made from cotton, besides those that are spoken of in this chapter.

A MALLOW PARTY

It would be a pleasant game to plan how to have a party with things to eat and things to wear from the cotton plant and other plants of the Mallow Family.

What could be used to thicken the soup? Name one vegetable that might be served. What sort of oil could be used for the salad? What sort of flour could there be in the bread? What would be used instead of butter? What sweet thing would you choose for dessert? What hot drink could there be instead of coffee?

If the dinner party were in a room that needed a light, there could be a lamp with cottonseed oil. (This kind of oil is used for burning in lamps in Russia and India. It is safer to use than kerosene.)

The invitations to the party could be written on paper made from the cotton stalk.

What kind of flowers would you choose to make the table look pretty?

What are some of the cotton things you could wear to such a party?

CHAPTER VII

FLAX AND SOME OTHER FIBER PLANTS

There are a great many kinds of plants with fibers that could be made into clothing if we needed to use them. If you were lost on an island where there were no stores, you could probably find something that could be woven if there were plants growing there. How would you know which things to use? Well, sometime when you are walking in the country you can play that you need to find something to weave so that you can have a blanket to wrap around you when your clothes wear out. Perhaps you will notice some dried and broken plant with string-like fibers that are tough enough to weave. There may be, at the edge of a pond, some stems that have broken off and are lying in the water; and perhaps you will find that you can strip out longer fibers from these wet stems than you can from dry ones. You may not be able to make very soft or very pretty cloth out of the things that you find that way. But if your eyes are as sharp at finding fibers to use as are those of an oriole (a beautiful bird that weaves a hanging nest), you can find different stringy bits that can be made into coarse cloth.

Long ago in hot climates where cotton plants grow, people found that the short fibers attached to cottonseed could be pulled off and twisted together into threads that could be woven into cloth.

An oriole makes a woven nest of fibers.

In places where pineapple plants grow, people found that fiber from the leaves could be used for making cloth. Some pineapple cloth is beautiful, and fine enough to make into thin handkerchiefs. This kind of cloth is made in the Philippine Islands.

People in the Philippine Islands make another kind of cloth from fibers they take from the stems of banana leaves. When you go there to visit you can buy some banana clothes and a pineapple handkerchief.

In Italy, straw braids for hats are made from wheat straw and from rye straw. When these plants are grown for such purposes, the seed is sown thickly and the plants are pulled up by the roots before the stems get too old to use. Barley and rice are grown in Japan and the stems are made into straw braid. The next time you buy a straw hat, try to find out at the store what kind of straw it is made with, and in what country the straw was grown.

Wheat and rye and barley and rice all belong to the Grass Family of plants. It is interesting to know that we eat the seeds and wear the stems of the same kinds of grass-like plants.

Of all the kinds of clothing that people have ever made from plants, the very oldest we know about is the kind that is made from fibers in the stem of the *flax* plant. We call this cloth *linen*.

Flax was grown in Egypt long ago in the time of Moses. Perhaps you have read about a hail storm that came and broke the herbs and trees.

> And the flax and the barley was smitten:
> For the barley was in the ear,
> And the flax was bolled.

(A boll, as we have seen, is a rounded seed pod. It is an old word, but we still use it when we speak of the cotton boll and the flax boll. It is really an old-fashioned way of spelling "bowl." The seed pods of some plants are rounded like little bowls. So when we say the flax "boll" we mean the little "bowl" in which the flax plant keeps its seeds.)

In the old days the royal princes of Egypt wore linen robes, and they made gifts of linen clothes to people they liked.

> And Pharaoh took off his ring from his hand,
> And put it upon Joseph's hand,
> And arrayed him in . . . fine linen,
> And put a gold chain about his neck.

116

If you read the history of the long-ago times in Egypt, you will notice that linen was looked upon as a very choice thing to wear. In those days in Egypt, the royal princes had linen robes while they lived. When they died, their bodies were wrapped tightly in linen cloth and placed in beautiful rooms in the pyramids. Such a body is now called a mummy. Many of the mummies have been taken out of the pyramids and put into museums so that we can see how they look and what treasures were buried with the old Egyptian princes.

So you need not even read history to learn about the old uses of linen, for you can see some of the linen cloth itself that was wrapped about a mummy a great many hundreds of years ago and has lasted all this long time. When you look at a piece of mummy cloth, you will think it wonderful that plant fiber can last so long without dropping to pieces.

Once upon a time there were some people living by the shores of the Red Sea who used to be fond of taking voyages in ships. They went to Egypt to trade with the Egyptians, and they saw the flax fields and the linen made from the flax fiber. It is thought that they took some of the flax seeds and carried them to Ireland. There are reasons for thinking that flax was grown in Ireland many years before it was known in Scotland and England.

Ireland has long been famous for its linen cloth. In an old book written about the time of Queen Elizabeth in England, there is a story about a man who made a trip into Ireland and found on his journey that "the Irish had such plenty of linen cloth that they wore thirty or forty ells in one shirt." When I tell you that an ell is longer than a yard, it will make you laugh to think of a shirt so big that it had thirty or forty ells of linen cloth in it.

When you go into a store and look at the handkerchiefs, you will find that some of them are labeled with the words "Pure Irish Linen." You will find, too, that there are a great many other things in the store made from Irish linen.

It is said that in one year alone enough linen cloth was woven in Ireland to make a path three feet wide around the earth. You can guess that so much linen cloth as that made a great many tablecloths and napkins and towels and dresses and handkerchiefs.

Indeed, so much cloth is woven in Irish mills that there is not enough flax grown in Ireland to make nearly all of it. Much of the flax fiber is taken there from other countries where it is grown.

You will remember that the cotton plant can grow only in hot climates where there is a long growing season. The flax plant is not like that. It can thrive in almost any climate that has about one hundred days warm enough to keep it alive from the time the seed sprouts until it grows up and has seeds of its own.

The flax plant has a stem from one to four feet high. Its branches are slender and its leaves are small and narrow. It has lovely bright blue flowers. A field of flax, when it is in blossom, is one of the most beautiful crops that a man can grow. Some people think that a flax field in flower is as lovely to look at as a field of grain with red poppies growing in it.

It used to be the custom in this country for every farmer to grow some flax on his own land. When the fiber was ready to use, the farmer's wife and daughters spun it into linen yarn. Perhaps you have seen an old spinning wheel that was used for this purpose. If you have never seen a real spinning wheel, perhaps you have seen a picture of one and know how it would look. The women used the linen yarn to weave into cloth for clothes and sheets and pillowcases and tablecloths and towels and kerchiefs to use in their own homes. In those days people grew their own cloth just as much as they did their own food.

A flax plant.

Later, when some of the farmers left the East and started to move west and kept going farther and farther, they found that flax was good to grow for their first crop after the prairie sod was plowed. Since there has been a great deal of prairie sod to plow up, there have been great fields of flax to sow and reap.

A field of flax in which the plants are being pulled carefully so that the fibers in the stems will not be broken.

You may wonder why, when so much flax is grown in America, we do not buy American linen in the stores instead of so much Irish linen. It is because in the United States more flax is raised for seed than for fiber. The flax seed, like the cotton seed, has a valuable oil in it, but it is put to different uses. The oil from flax seeds is called *linseed oil* and is used in paint and varnish.

Linseed oil is used in other ways, too. Perhaps you can learn about some of the other uses of this kind of oil. After the oil has been pressed out of the seeds, the meal that is left is sold as food for farm animals.

When flax is grown for the seed crop, it can be cut with the same sort of machines that are used in grain fields, and the seeds can be threshed out with ordinary threshing machines. It does not cost a great deal to harvest flax seeds in this way.

When the flax is harvested for its fiber to be used for cloth, great care is needed in handling the plants. It is best, then, to pull them up by hand so that the fiber may be as long as possible. The fiber is in one layer of the bark on the stem, and it cannot be separated easily unless the stem is soaked in water until parts of the stem are soft. This is called rotting, or *retting*, the flax. The stems are left in a wet field or put into a stream or pool of water. Great numbers of little bacteria grow in the wet flax and help rot or soften the parts of the plant that hold the fibers together. After the stems have been

This picture shows how flax is retted in Belgium. The plants are packed in great open crates in the river, which are held down by stones.

retted, the fibers are separated from the other parts of the stem by machinery. The fibers are usually from one to three feet long, depending on how high the plants grew and how carefully the stems have been handled.

The best fibers are used for cloth. The coarser, poorer fibers are made into rope and string or used for stuffing furniture and other things that need to be padded. Sometimes, even when flax is grown for seed, the stems can be used, too, for things that do not need a good kind of fiber.

A FLAX GAME

Here is a pleasant game. See if some of the children in your class can bring a flower catalog to school. Look to see if you can find pictures of flax in it. One catalog that I looked at has a colored picture of crimson flax. Another catalog that I saw offers to sell seeds of pink and scarlet and yellow and white and blue flax, some for five cents a package.

These flax seeds are for flower gardens and the plants that grow from them have bigger blossoms than the plants that are grown for fiber and linseed oil. But they are all closely related to the blue flax in the farmers' fields; and it would be fun for you to grow some of them and notice whether the leaves of the different kinds of flax plants are narrow and the stems and branches slender like those of the flax plants that are grown in fields. It would be fun, too, for you to notice how long one blossom lasts; how many weeks or days or hours it is from the time one bud opens until the petals drop off. It would be fun to find out whether the seed pods of the different kinds are rounded so that they can be called bolls. It would be fun to soak some of the stems in water to see if you can find any fibers in the bark.

If there is a school garden at your school, perhaps you will be allowed to grow a few flax plants there. If you have a yard at home, perhaps there will be a place where you can grow a little flax to see how it looks.

Perhaps you will need to wait until you are grown up and have a garden of your own before you can grow red and white and blue flax. These flowers are pretty enough to be worth waiting for.

CHAPTER VIII

SPINNERS OF SILK

There are so many spinners of silk in the world that any boy or girl, by hunting about, can find one of them to watch.

SPIDERS

Spiders spin silk. Some line the walls of their caves with silk. Some make wonderful traps of silk, their webs, in which to catch their food. Webs are most beautiful to look at in the early morning when there is a little dew on them so that the fine silken lines are easy to see. Some spiders spin firm silken bags in which to keep their eggs until they hatch.

Some spiders spin silk to help them travel through the air. You know that the seeds of some plants, such as milkweed and cotton and dandelion and many others, journey through the air by means of fine fibers that are on the seeds. Such seeds are carried through the air by the wind. Some kinds of spiders go sailing through the air in much the same way.

When such a spider is ready to take an air trip, it

climbs up high on something, as the tip of a branch, or the top of a post, or as far as it can get on some plant that is near. Then it sticks the tip of its body into the air and begins to spin.

Spider web spun with spider silk.

The silk is a sticky sort of fluid while it is in the spider's body, but when it touches the air it hardens into silken fiber. The wind blows against the fiber and the spider lets more and more silk come out of its body, making the fiber longer and longer. The longer it gets, the harder the wind pushes against it.

Did you ever fly a kite and feel the wind tug against it until it pulls so strongly that you find you can hardly hold the kite? Then you unroll more and more string from the ball so that the kite can go farther and farther away into the air. If you were not so heavy, the wind could lift you up and off you would go, kite and all! That is what happens to the spider. After a while, when the silken fiber is long and the push of the wind against it is strong, the spider lets go its hold on the branch or post or plant tip and goes off with the wind, hanging to its own kite string.

Spiders ready to take a trip through the air. They sail at the end of a long silken "kite string" which they spin.

It is usually very young spiders that go kiting around that way. They have eight little legs on which to travel, but they can get somewhere faster by going on a kite string. If they can go away from the place where their mother hunted, perhaps they will find more food when they are ready to settle down. You will remember that some kinds of baby plants, while they are seeds, sail off in much the same way and find places to live in that are not too near the old plants of the same kind.

Long ago men learned how to use spider silk to weave into cloth. When they first tried to do this, they tore up the bags the spiders made for their eggs and wove cloth with the torn bits. But now people have a way of getting spider silk without breaking the fibers into short lengths.

If you travel to the Indian Ocean some time and visit an island in that ocean, perhaps you can see for yourself how men now get spider silk to use. Since it may be a long time before you go so far as that, I will tell you a little about it now. Spiders of a certain kind are put into wee stalls which hold them in place without hurting them. Then the spiders begin to spin and the silken fibers come out of their bodies. The fibers from a number of spiders are caught together on a little tool and twisted into a thread that is large and strong enough to wind on a reel. Soft and beautiful cloth is woven from such spider silk.

Caterpillars

Caterpillars of almost all kinds spin some silk. Some kinds spin only a few inches of fibers and some kinds spin fibers that are hundreds of feet long.

There are two *silk glands* inside the body of the caterpillar; and these connect and have an opening through the lower lip of the caterpillar. It is out of this opening that the silk comes. While silk is inside the silk glands it is a liquid, but when it touches the air it becomes stiffened into a thread.

Some kinds of caterpillars begin to spin the very same day they hatch. Caterpillars hatch out of eggs that moths or butterflies lay, so they are really baby moths or butterflies although they do not look a bit like their fathers and mothers. That is, they do not until they are grown up, and by that time they are not caterpillars any more. When they are grown up, they are moths or butterflies themselves and have four wings and six legs; and they can do many things they cannot do while they are caterpillars. But they cannot spin any more silk. They can spin silk only while they are caterpillars.

Perhaps some day when you are walking near an apple or other kind of tree you may see a caterpillar spin a silken "life line." Suddenly a little caterpillar comes down, dropping off a leaf when the branch is jarred. But it does not fall all the way to the ground, and this is the reason. It sticks a bit of silk to the leaf before it drops, and then it spins as it falls. So there it swings in the air, sometimes several feet below the branch. The silken thread that holds it is so fine that you can hardly see it, and yet it is strong enough to hold the caterpillar's body. When the caterpillar drops down far enough, it stops spinning and swings at the end of its life line until everything seems quiet again.

Then if you are not silly and say, "Oh, what a horrid little worm!" and run away, you can have the fun of watching the little caterpillar do something very wonderful. It will begin to creep up its life line to the leaf, and it will take the silk up with it. On the part of the body near the head there are three pairs of legs. The caterpillar uses these legs like hands in climbing up the life line "hand over hand." It uses these legs like hands, too, in winding the silk line into a little ball as it goes up. At least a kind that I have watched does this. What it does with this little ball of silk when it gets back to the leaf, I do not know. Do you suppose it keeps its little ball of silk and unwinds it, using the same line over again the next time a child or a bird or something else jars against the branch? That would be a good thing for you to watch and find out for yourself.

Caterpillar at the end of "life line." How will it get back to the leaf?

Tent caterpillars spin a silken tent which serves for shelter at night and when the days are rainy. All the brother and sister caterpillars that hatch out of one batch of eggs live together in the same tent. At first the

129

caterpillars are very small, and the tent, to begin with, is a tiny one started in the place where two branches of a tree grow apart. In the warm part of the day, they go out of the tent and wander along a branch until they come to some leaves. Then they eat until it is time for them to go back to their tent for the night. The more leaves they eat, the bigger they grow; so they need to keep spinning more silk to make the tent large enough to cover them.

A tent caterpillar stays inside its tent while it molts, or sheds its skin. A caterpillar does not have any bones to keep its body firm. The skin is the firmest part of the body and is a sort of skeleton which it wears on the outside. When its skin gets too tight, it splits open down the back like a rip in a seam, and then the caterpillar crawls out through the ripped place. Its new skin stretches enough so that the caterpillar can grow one size larger before it needs to molt again. A caterpillar needs a quiet place while it is molting, and a tent is a very good home at such a time.

Caterpillars that do not live in tents often spin thin silk mats just before it is time for them to change their skins. They tangle the claws of their creeping feet into the fibers of the mats, and then they do not fall while they are molting.

Certain caterpillars do not get their growth before winter comes, so they must wait until spring before there are any more leaves for them to eat.

Some caterpillars spin snug winter nests and sleep in them all winter without eating. You may find a whole family of brother and sister caterpillars working together to make a firm nest, which they fasten to the branch of a tree. They fix little silken rooms in the winter nest and snuggle up close together while they take their long nap. In the spring, when the leaves are fresh and tender, the young caterpillars waken. Then they go out and eat greedily enough to make up for all the long wait between their fall supper and their spring breakfast.

There is one time in its life when almost every kind of caterpillar spins some silk. That time is after it has eaten its very last caterpillar meal and has become as large as it can grow. Then it must

Silken nest which a family of young caterpillars has spun for a winter home.

stop being a caterpillar and turn into a *pupa*. (Pupa is what an insect is called while it is resting and waiting for its wings to grow.) A pupa is a quiet, helpless thing that cannot eat or spin or walk about, and a caterpillar needs to get ready to be a pupa by taking care of itself beforehand.

Some caterpillars get ready by spinning little silken pegs to hang on while they are waiting for their wings to grow. Some get ready by burying themselves in the ground, where they hollow out little caves in which to rest. But many caterpillars get ready by spinning *cocoons*, in which they wait for their wings to grow.

A cocoon is the silken room the caterpillar spins when it is through with its leaf-eating, growing days and is ready to change into a moth. It cannot suddenly molt its caterpillar skin and be a moth. That is too quick a change for its body to make. There must be time for the insect to be made over from a creeping caterpillar to a flying moth. This change takes place while it is a pupa.

It is a great event to get ready to be a pupa. It takes the very best a caterpillar can do to fix a safe place in which to rest, and nothing can be better for such a nap than a cocoon.

The caterpillar does not wind the silk about itself as if it were a ball. It swings its head with a slow, steady motion, while the silk comes out of the opening through its lower lip as a very fine fiber. It holds its head up and guides the silk with its little hand-like feet that are near the head. No one can see a caterpillar start its cocoon without having something wonderful to remember. It is usually only the beginning of a cocoon that can be watched; for after the outside is made the caterpillar is covered, and as the wall gets thicker less and less can be seen. Each kind of caterpillar makes its own kind of cocoon.

Cecropia

The name of the biggest kind of caterpillar living in many parts of this country is *Cecropia*. By the time it is ready to spin its cocoon it may be nearly four inches long, and it is a handsome creature. It is hard to tell whether its body is blue or green, so we will call it blue-green. It is trimmed with red and blue and yellow things that are shaped like pegs with points on them.

A Cecropia caterpillar makes two cocoons, one inside the other, like puzzle boxes. There is a doorway leading out of the cocoon, but it is a secret sort of doorway. It does not show from the outside and the more it is pushed against from the outside, the tighter it closes. But a very little pushing from the inside opens the doorway. The Cecropia stays inside this safe place and molts its last caterpillar skin. Then it is not a gay-colored caterpillar any more. It is an oval brown pupa, which rests in its snug double chamber of silk all winter. This double cocoon is fastened to the under side of a branch and it looks something like a little gray or brown hammock tapered at both ends.

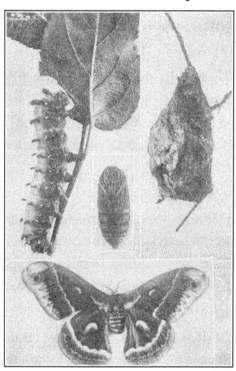

The Cecropia, a giant silkworm. When the caterpillar is nearly four inches long, it stops eating leaves and spins a cocoon (upper right). Inside the cocoon, it changes to a brown pupa (center). In the spring the pupa becomes a moth, which creeps out of the cocoon and flies away when night comes.

133

In the spring, after it has become a moth and has broken out of the brown skin it wore while it was a pupa, the Cecropia comes creeping out through the secret doorway. Its body is plump, and its wings are limp little flaps. These flaps soon expand into fully spread wings that are about six inches from tip to tip. The colors of the wings are lovely shades of soft brown with trimmings of white and rich red.

The Cecropia caterpillar is one of the *giant silkworms*. There is so much strong silk fiber in its cocoon that people have tried to unwind it and weave it into cloth. Each fiber breaks at the doorway, however, so this kind of cocoon is troublesome to unwind.

There are other giant silkworms in this country just as handsome as the Cecropia, though their colors are different and they are not so large. They change into moths that are just as beautiful as the Cecropia. Some of them spin cocoons that are whole, with no doorway left in them. These cocoons, if softened, can be unwound and the silk used for cloth.

It is, indeed, from the cocoons of certain giant silkworms in some parts of the world that some of the silk is unwound that people use for cloth. This is called *wild silk*, because the giant silkworms are left "wild" on the trees and their cocoons are found wherever they happen to be. Some wild silk is gathered in China and Japan, and a great deal is taken in India. If you can get someone to show you a piece of real *pongee*, you will know how cloth made from wild silk looks.

The Silkworm

Most of the real silk cloth in the world is made from the fiber that is spun by one kind of "tame" caterpillar. This is called the *Chinese silkworm* or the *mulberry silkworm* or just the *silkworm*.

Caterpillar, cocoon, and moth of the Chinese silkworm among mulberry leaves.

The silkworm's skin is smooth and yellowish white. This caterpillar likes the leaves of the *mulberry tree* better than any other food. When it has eaten as many mulberry leaves as it can, it is about two inches long, and it is then ready to spin its cocoon. Its cocoon is yellow or white and it is spun with unbroken fiber and without any doorway.

The silkworm lives as a pupa inside the cocoon for

about three weeks (or more if it is kept in a cool place), and by the end of that time it has its wings and is ready to come out of the cocoon. Although the cocoon has no doorway, the moth has a way of coming out. It squirts some liquid against one end of the cocoon. This liquid softens the gum that holds the silk together. It is then easy for the moth to push its way out through the wet end of the cocoon. The moth is cream-colored, with some faint brown lines on the forewings.

There are many interesting stories about this important insect. Long, long ago the Chinese people found out that if they put the cocoons of the mulberry caterpillars into hot water, the gummy stuff on the silk would soften and the fiber could be unwound. They found that fibers from several of these cocoons could be twisted together into thread and then woven into cloth.

One story is that the Empress Si-Ling-Chi was the first to rear the caterpillars and reel silk from the cocoons, and she was given great honor and called "Goddess of the Silkworm." This way of getting silk fiber to use was kept a secret by the Chinese. They practiced weaving and dyeing and embroidering until they could make wonderful silk cloth with pictures of flowers and dragons and people on it. The silk robes that the Chinese princes wore were the most beautiful in all the world.

The Chinese sold some of their silk cloth to travelers from other countries, who paid great prices for it. This cloth was so famous that China was called "Land of Silk."

People from other countries could buy all the silk cloth they could afford, but they could not buy the thread or find out where it came from. That was a secret that the Chinese kept for many hundreds of years. No one in China dared to tell about it. If anyone was found trying to take eggs of the silkworm moths out of China, he was put to death. If people in other countries wanted silk thread to use, they had to ravel it out of the silk cloth that came from China. Some of them thought that this thread came from a plant, as linen and cotton do. Some thought that it was made from the fleece of sheep in a secret way.

There is a story that at last a Roman emperor hired two monks to go to China as spies and learn the secret of silk. These monks traveled on foot to China, where they watched and found out how the silkworms were cared for and how the cocoons were thrown into hot water and the silk taken off on reels. Then they stuffed their hollow canes with eggs of the silkworm moths and escaped back to the Roman emperor, who put them in charge of making silk in his country.

In one way and another the secret of getting silk at last reached the people living in the different countries. Mulberry trees were planted in many places where they had never grown before, and their leaves were stripped off and fed to the tame silkworms.

When James I was King of England, he sent some mulberry trees and silkworm eggs to Virginia and told the people there to raise silk instead of tobacco. So they did as they were told for a while.

Sometime when you are a little older you can have a pleasant time reading different stories of how people tried to raise silkworms in America. You will read that Benjamin Franklin wished to get the people in Pennsylvania to grow silkworms. In many other states, too, people tried; and for a while it was the fashion for American ladies to wear silk gowns made from silk they had unwound from the cocoons of silkworms they had taken care of themselves. Perhaps sometime you will want to find out whether the silkworms were ever grown in your state. In most parts of this country people gave up trying. But if you happen to live in California, you may like to know that only a few years ago a man living there planted many thousands of mulberry trees for silkworm food.

Although few people in the United States are now interested in growing silkworms, more silk is woven into cloth in American mills than in the mills of any other country. Where are the silkworms that spin all this silk? Most of them live in China and Japan and Italy, and the silk is sent over here to be woven after it has been unwound from the cocoons.

ARTIFICIAL SILK

There are some kinds of cloth and neckties and stockings that look like silk although they are not made from silkworm silk. We call this "artificial silk." The story of how this material is made is a very interesting one; but it does not belong in this book. Now that you have finished a chapter about real silk, it would be a good time for you to try to find out a little about artificial silk, if you can find someone who will tell you.

CHAPTER IX

FUR COATS AND ANIMALS THAT WEAR THEM

SHEEP

If you have ever had a coat of woolen cloth, you have worn a sort of fur coat. The animal that wore your coat first was a sheep. The sheep's hair was cut off its body and spun into yarn and then woven into the cloth used in making your coat.

You have read about cloth made of cotton fiber and flax fiber and silk fiber. The hair of sheep is another kind of fiber that can be made into cloth.

The hair of sheep is usually called *wool*.

A fiber of wool has little scales on it. These scales are so small that you cannot see them unless you look through a microscope. When the wool is spun into yarn, the little scales on one hair catch and tangle into those of other hairs. The scales hold the fibers together and make the yarn strong.

There was a time long ago when people did not know how to weave cloth. In those days people who lived in cold places and needed warm clothing wore the skins of animals.

The hair in your woolen clothes was first worn by sheep. This picture shows how wool is sheared from sheep. On small farms, it is cut off with hand shears. On large ranches, the shears are run by machinery.

Some of the animals that people killed and skinned were sheep. The skins were scraped on the inside and dried and then worn, skin and hair and all. Sheep fur made such good warm clothing that people have kept on using it from that day to this. Even after men learned how to shear the wool from the live sheep once a year and make it into cloth, they still kept on killing some of the sheep and using the skin, hair and all, for fur.

A black lamb with a beautiful curly fur coat.

Some sheep fur is used for lining coats which are worn with the fur inside. Some lambs have very beautiful curly fur that is not used for lining but for the outside of the coat where it shows.

We do not know when people began to keep flocks of sheep, but we know that it was long ago indeed. There have been many interesting stories about sheep and the shepherds who took care of them, and some of these stories are very old. But there was a time when sheep were wild and went their own way without any help or care from men. They went together for company in wild flocks. Their flesh was good to eat and their fur was warm to wear, and men began, after a while, to keep such flocks near them where they could be caught at any time. It was easier to take care of the tame animals than to hunt for the wild ones.

In many states, small flocks of sheep are kept in fenced pastures. They like some plants that cows will not eat; and sometimes, after the cows have fed on the grass in a pasture, sheep are put in to feed on plants that are left.

In the West, millions of sheep are allowed to feed in the National Forests each summer. It is said that in some places such flocks of sheep have eaten so much that the wild deer in the forests have been hungry.

FOXES

There are fox farms, though these are much newer than sheep farms. Foxes cannot be herded in flocks on a farm, because it is not their nature to live together in large numbers for company when they are wild.

Wild father and mother foxes and their little ones live in one family; and when the young ones grow up and have learned to hunt for themselves, each one must go away and have a home of his own. Foxes are hunters, and most kinds of hunters like best to go alone when they hunt.

Did you ever notice how much braver a dog is in his own yard than he is in other places? Foxes seem to have a feeling that they have a right to hunt and play in the woods and fields near where they live and that others of their kinds (even their own grown children) ought to stay away.

A tame fox that liked to run to some high place and look far off.

Of course foxes, feeling as they do about such matters, cannot be expected to herd together like sheep in a flock. They need their own yards and their own dens to live in, even when they are kept on a farm. Foxes are timid, but if their caretaker understands how to treat animals so as to make friends with them, they like his kindness.

When it is time to kill tame foxes for their fur, this can be done quickly and in a way that does not give pain, as traps do to wild foxes. When wild foxes are killed, it is often at times when their skins and hair are not good for fur. On a fox farm the tame foxes are killed only when their fur is good enough to use.

If there were enough fox farms, wild foxes might have a pleasanter time than they do now because people might let them alone in the woods and fields and such free places as they choose for their own yards. Wild foxes sometimes help themselves to hens and geese and turkeys, if people are shiftless and do not build the right sort of poultry houses or fences. Since rats and certain other animals like chickens, too, henhouses and yards should be built to keep poultry inside and other animals outside, even if there were no foxes.

SKUNKS

Did you ever see a skunk? People do not think that "skunk" is a pretty name, but the animal the name belongs to is very handsome indeed.

One day I saw some little skunk kittens in an oak grove, and they were so playful that it was fun to watch them. Once in a forest I saw a grown skunk hunting. He ran to a soft old stump and tore it to bits with his front paws. He looked very quickly to see what insects he could find, and then hurried away to another stump.

One morning about sunrise I saw some skunks hunting on a prairie field. The grass on the prairie was brown and dry. Some underground insects had chewed off the roots, so of course the grass died. But the skunks came into the field and ate the insects before they could go into another field and kill any more grass. These skunks had a good way of hunting, and they were funny to watch. They ripped places in the dry sod with their claws and then rolled it back out of the way like strips of rolled carpet. That made it easy for them to find the juicy insects in the ground.

Skunks like grass-eating insects better than they do chickens. In some states the farmers know this and have laws to prevent men from killing skunks. It is easier and cheaper for men to build good henhouses to keep out skunks and rats and foxes than it is for them to kill some of the insects that eat valuable crops. Since skunks help the farmers take care of their crops, it is only fair for men to make laws to protect the skunks.

Skunks are not timid. Even the wild ones are not. The reason they are not timid is that they have a very good way of taking care of themselves. There are two scent glands in their bodies under the skin, one on each side, near the base of the tail. These scent glands are little sacs filled with liquid. When skunks are attacked or badly frightened, they squirt out the liquid from their scent sacs in two streams of fine spray. It is not a pleasant-smelling scent. In fact it smells bad enough to make people or dogs or other animals feel sick if they try to bother skunks.

Since a skunk can make animals sick if they try to harm it, it does not need to be timid. It does not need to run to its home like a fox. It does not need to hide at all. It can walk about slowly and show its pretty black and white coat plainly.

Did you ever see a handsome black and white animal like this? Some people call it a wood pussy, and some people call it a skunk.

Early one morning I met a skunk in a path. He was not a tame skunk, but he was not afraid. I walked up the path until I was not far from the skunk. He did not run away. He patted the ground with his front paws and then he lifted his tail. His tail was a signal of danger when he lifted it like that. He was not horrid about it. He was quite polite. He gave me a chance to stop where I was. I stopped. Then I went backwards very slowly until I was far enough away to suit the pretty black and white animal. In a minute he lowered his tail and went on with his walk up the path. I sniffed the air and there was not even one little bit of skunk scent. All he wanted was a chance to go walking without having anyone come too near.

Since skunks are not naturally timid, they are easy to tame. In fact, even the wild ones like being near places where people live. They like to stay under barns and sheds. They like such places for shelter for themselves and their young. There is another reason why they come to barns and sheds. They are glad to eat rats and mice and are pleased to come where they can find them. People who know about this sometimes have tame skunks for mouse-catchers. Some people get young skunks and take out the scent sacs, and then let them run about the house as much as they like. It is not necessary to take out these sacs, since tame skunks soon learn to know their friends. But most people feel safer to have the scent glands out of the way, so that there may be no bad-smelling accident if a stranger should come into the house and be rude to the skunks.

A girl once told me about a pet skunk she had. She

found it caught with its foot in a trap and she felt sorry. So she took it out of the trap and put it into an empty henhouse. She knew how to hold it so that it could not spray her. She gave it good food and fresh water and kept it shut up until it knew her and liked to be handled. This pet soon found that it was fun to climb up and take a ride on the girl's shoulders. The henhouse was a lonesome place and the little animal was very happy when the girl would let it go into the house for a visit. When the girl's father was resting on the sofa, the skunk would climb up and curl down cosily beside him and have a nap, too. The scent glands of this skunk were not removed, but the pet never did any harm about the house and was not bad-smelling at all.

The fur of skunks is warm and good and people wear it. You may think that, since skunks are easily tamed, they can be kept on a fur farm. So they can. They are less work to care for than foxes are, but their fur does not sell for so much money.

MUSKRATS

There is a kind of fur farm where muskrats live. Muskrats do not need to be shut up inside of pens and fences. People who want a muskrat farm need only to buy or rent a marsh where land is cheap and let the muskrats take care of themselves. They do not even need to be fed, for there are enough plants in the marsh for them to eat.

Muskrats on a fur farm dig their own tunnels and build their own winter houses and have altogether a good time as long as they live. When it is time to catch some of them for their fur, if this is done in the right kind of water-traps, the muskrats drown so quickly that they do not suffer.

A muskrat stays where it can find water plants to eat.

A muskrat is not the dirty brown rat that comes into houses and barns for grain and other food that we need to use. A muskrat grows to be about four times as large as a common brown rat, and it lives in and near the water. Its tail is flattened sidewise and makes a good, long rudder when the muskrat swims. Its fur is thick and waterproof so that the muskrat can swim without being soaked.

Muskrats do not sleep the winter away as do some animals that live in the North. So they need food to eat even when the ground is covered with snow and the marsh water has a roof of ice. If they live where there are banks to dig in, they often make caves and live in them in winter as well as in summer. The door-holes of these caves are under water, so it is easy for the muskrats to swim out when they are hungry for roots and stems of such plants as they like to eat.

In the North where it is very cold in winter, muskrats build houses in the fall, unless they find very good banks for caves. They build houses of water grasses and stems and roots of other plants that they like to eat. They pile the roots, dirt and all, on the outside of their houses, and the dirt helps to plaster the houses and keep them warm. These busy animals heap the houses higher and higher until at last the buildings stick up out of the water for two or three feet. Then they dig out a room inside each house and make passageways

Northern muskrats build houses in which to spend the winter.

down into the water below danger of freezing. In the winter, on days when it seems too cold to pull fresh food, the muskrats eat some of the stems and roots that are in the thick walls of their houses.

Perhaps you know that people have another use for muskrats than merely their fur. Muskrat meat is good to eat. At the meat markets it is often called "marsh rabbit"; and this is the name, too, people often use when they ask for muskrat meat at hotels. When it is properly prepared and cooked, muskrat meat has a taste that people like very much. It can be fried or roasted or stewed.

SOME OTHER ANIMALS WITH FUR COATS

It would take a whole big book to tell about all the animals that wear fur coats. There is room for only a few in one chapter. You will find something about the bear and the beaver and some of the others in different chapters in this book. You can think of still others for yourself. Some of the furs that people wear come from animals that you know very well, such as cats and dogs and squirrels and rabbits.

You know that all animals, even cats and dogs and cows, went their own wild ways once upon a time, very long ago indeed. If foxes and skunks and beavers and other wild animals are kept on fur farms for hundreds of years, do you suppose that they will not seem like "wild" animals any more?

You may wonder why there are so few wild animals in our forests and along our streams, in places where there were once so many of them. One reason is that people have killed great numbers of fur animals at times when their fur is not good. There are only a few months each year when fur is good enough for people to use. Another reason is that many places have been changed so that animals cannot live there, by draining swamps and drying out the water that the wild animals need, and by cutting down forests, and by plowing prairies, and by building cities.

Still another reason why there are not more wild animals is that many of the laws that are supposed to protect fur animals are not wise ones, because people have not always understood enough about what really ought to be done. It is not enough just to want to do what is best for animal friends. Lawmakers should know how to do it the best way. You will be old enough some day to help make the laws for your state and your country; and it is not too soon for you to begin to learn about the animals that will be in your care, so that you will know what is the fair and kind way to treat them.

How to take care of wild animals is a very important matter indeed. You will not be able to think it all out by yourself; but it is something you can talk over with your schoolmates, and with older friends too. You may not know the answers to all the questions at the close of this chapter, now; but if you begin to think about them to-day, some day you may know enough about them to help make wiser and better laws than we have now.

In National Forests where wild deer live, do you think men should be allowed to put so many sheep that the deer suffer from hunger because the sheep have eaten the food?

Do you think that there should be laws against catching animals in the kinds of traps that cause them pain?

Do people need to wear fur in summer? Do they need fur trimming on sunshades? When do people really need fur?

Do you know the name of one kind of fur-coated animal that lives wild in your state?

CHAPTER X

FEATHERS AND ANIMALS THAT WEAR THEM

BIDDY, THE PET HEN

She had a nest so cosy
  With twelve eggs in it, too.
I helped her keep her secret
  And not a body knew.

Sometimes when she was thirsty
  I filled her water cup,
And when I took her corn to eat
  She swallowed it all up.

She knew just how to thank me
  By croaking in her throat.
But if I touched her eggs a bit,
  She had a crosser note,

And made her feathers ruffled
  As pussy does her fur—
A way she had to tell me
  Those eggs belonged to her.

At last I heard some peeping
  And then, oh, oh, oh, oh!
Her darling little chickens
  Were cuddled up just so!

Did you ever have a pet hen?

A FLOCK OF TURKEYS

Once there was a turkey gobbler who used to bring his flock of turkey hens to visit in our yard. Their home was on a farm a mile away, but they liked to walk across the fields and eat grasshoppers as they came.

The gobbler was fond of strutting with his tail spread like a fan. He acted as if he were pleased with the way his feathers looked.

He would fly up to the top of a high post and then look down at all the turkey hens and talk to them. The hens would stand on the ground and look up at him as if they liked to hear what he said. Perhaps they knew what he meant by his queer sounds.

When the gobbler was ready to go home again, the whole flock would go with him. Sometimes they flew up into the branches of trees to spend the night. They liked branches much better than roosts in a house.

The turkey hens had hidden nests, where they went when they laid their eggs. They never cackled or made any sound to tell where their nests were. The eggs were large and they had pretty speckles on the shells. When there were enough eggs in the nests, the mother turkeys would sit on them for four weeks. It took all that time for the bodies of the baby turkeys inside the eggs to grow. The mother turkeys were patient and stayed on the eggs night and day, leaving them only when they needed a few minutes to get food or water.

A turkey gobbler likes a post where he can stand up high and look about.

At the end of four weeks, when the baby turkeys inside the shells were big and strong enough to come out, they rapped against the inside of the shells with their bills until the shells broke. As soon as their feathers dried, the turkey chicks were pretty, downy little things. They did not need to stay in the nest as some baby birds do. They could run about at once as soon as they were hungry, and find small insects and pick up food the farmer put on the ground.

ROBINS

People must buy their hens and geese and ducks and turkeys if they wish to keep those birds. But there are some kinds of birds that people need not buy in order to have them near. *Robins* often make their nests where it is easy for people to give them protection.

The robins I knew best, when I was a little girl, were some that built their nest on a high step of a big wagon. It was a good thing for the birds that the farmer who owned the wagon was kind-hearted, for he found a way to get along without using the wagon until the robins left it.

The father and mother robins brought some mud in their mouths and made the nest mostly of that. Mud was not the only stuff they used. They took, too, dead grass in the morning when it was wet with dew and could be bent without breaking. The wet grass helped hold the mud together.

The mother robin went inside the nest and pressed her body against the mud while it was damp and soft. She turned around and around in it and pressed it with her breast. Some of the mud made her feathers dirty; but that did no harm, for as soon as the mud was dry she shook it off and was clean again.

The nest was lined with soft dead grass, and when it was dry the mother robin laid a blue egg in it. Every day she laid an egg until she had four. Then she began to stay on the nest to keep the eggs warm. When she needed to be away from the nest, the father robin stayed on it. If the eggs had been left long enough to get cold, the baby robins inside the shells could not have grown.

After the eggs had been kept warm for two weeks, the young birds broke the shells. The next thing they did was to open their mouths for food. They opened their mouths so much that I felt sorry for the old birds and thought I would try to help them.

I soaked some bread in milk and put it on the wagon step near the nest. In a little while I looked and found that the bread was gone. I put a piece on the steps every few hours and every time I went the old piece would be gone. I thought I was helping very nicely, but every time I took out some bread the mother bird scolded me. Each time I left her some bread she was crosser to me than she had been the time before. At last I hid behind the shed door and looked through a crack to watch her. I thought she would feed the bread to the baby robins. But she did not. She left her nest with an angry jerk and picked up the wet bread in her bill and flew off a little way and dropped it on the ground.

After that I did not try to help the robins feed their young. They found plenty of earthworms and caterpillars for their four greedy youngsters, who all grew up to be strong and healthy and left the nest before they could fly very well.

The old robins did not have speckles on their breasts.

They had plain red breasts. But the four young birds had speckled breasts.

There is a family of birds called the Thrush Family. Most of the thrushes have speckles on their breasts. Robins belong to this family of birds, and their very first suits of feathers always have speckles in front. There are some young robins in the last picture in this book.

BLUEBIRDS

You may call *bluebirds* cousins to the robins, because bluebirds belong to the Thrush Family, too. An old father bluebird has a blue back and a reddish breast, but the young bluebirds have spotted fronts on their first suits.

Bluebirds often come to live next door to people if they can find trees with hollows in them or bird boxes in which to build their nests.

Like other members of the Thrush Family, the bluebirds go south for the winter, but sometimes they fly north again in the spring so early that there may still be snow on the ground.

One cold spring morning a girl who lives in the North heard a bluebird singing its sweet soft song. The girl said joyfully, "The bluebirds have come! The bluebirds are here!" Then she looked at the ground all covered with snow and felt sorry because it would be hard for the bluebirds to find any insects. So she thought she would give them something else to eat. She nailed a short board shelf to the trunk of a tree near the house and put some peanut butter on the shelf. Then she went into the house and watched through the window. In a little while the bluebirds flew to the shelf and ate peanut butter.

There was a bird box in the same tree; and later, when the weather was warm and sunny, the bluebirds made their nest in the box. That was a rather cold, rainy summer; and after the young bluebirds were hatched, the old birds often had to hunt in the rain for food for their family.

On such days the girl remembered to put peanut butter on the shelf and the father and mother birds came down to the food and ate it very gladly. One rainy day, after the young birds were out of their nest and could fly, the girl put peanut butter on the shelf. After a while the old birds coaxed their young ones to the shelf and fed them all. This sort of food must have been good for the bluebirds, for they seemed to be well and happy.

In October when the maple trees were wearing their brightest yellow and red colors, it was time for the bluebirds to fly to the South. One day some bluebirds flew into the girl's yard. There were a father and mother bluebird and four young ones. They all went to the box near the shelf and hopped in and out of the round doorway in the box. They made cheerful singing sounds. The girl thought that they were the same birds that had eaten her peanut butter and that they had come to say good-by to the home where they had had a good time.

Tree Swallows

Tree swallows are pretty little birds with shining bluish-green feathers above and white ones beneath. They like such boxes for nests as bluebirds do.

If tree swallows ever come to live in your bird box, you can have a pleasant time when they are building their nest. These birds like soft, fluffy white feathers for their nests better than anything else. If you put some white feathers on the ground, they will fly down and get them. If you hold a fluffy white feather high in your hand and keep still, the birds will fly near and try to get it. If you let go of the feather, the birds will catch it before it reaches the ground. Then, when they are used to coming near, you can keep hold of a feather until the birds are brave enough to come and pick it out of your fingers. They will not sit on your hand while they do this, but catch the feather with their bills as they fly.

Swallows are used to getting their food, too, as they fly, and they catch flying insects for themselves and for their young birds.

English Sparrows

There was a time, less than one hundred years ago, when there were no *English sparrows* in this country. These birds lived in Europe, where they are called "house sparrows," which is a very good name for them because they come to cities where houses are thick. They like the same nesting places that bluebirds and tree swallows do, and often drive these other birds away. They do not really need the boxes and hollow trees that these other birds like, because they can build in any sheltered place about a house that has room for a nest.

Many people do not like English sparrows at all, but some people like them and feed them. Perhaps if you watch them and listen to them, you can find out whether you think they are as nice as other birds. If you live in a city, you will see more English sparrows than if your home is in the country. When you learn about them and their habits, you can tell whether you think it was a good plan to bring such birds here from Europe.

THE SMALLEST BIRD

The smallest birds of all are the *hummingbirds*. The common kind in the United States is three and one half inches long. The father hummingbird has a shining green back and the feathers underneath are a soft sort of gray. At his throat are some feathers that gleam in the sunlight like a red jewel. This kind of hummingbird is called the *rubythroat*. The mother bird has about the same sort of suit except that she has no bright color at her throat.

If you wish to see some ruby-throated humming-birds, the best way to do it is to spend as much time as you can near some red flowers. These hummingbirds visit certain flowers of other colors, also, but red flowers are the ones that seem to please them best of all. They fly to wild flowers, but they are not too timid to come to flower gardens. They will even fly to porches and window boxes that have red geraniums in them.

A hummingbird has a long, slender bill that it can poke into deep flowers. It likes to drink the sweet nectar that is in flowers. It likes, too, the tiny insects that it finds there. A hummingbird's wings move so quickly that they make a little humming sound. After one has been flying about on humming wings for a while, it leaves its flowery feast and rests quietly on some tiny twig. I have often seen a hummingbird come back again and again to the same twig to rest between meals.

The ruby-throated hummingbird is the only kind of hummingbird in the United States east of the Rocky Mountains. In Mexico and in the warmest parts of South America there are many kinds of hummingbirds, with brilliant colors.

In the winter the ruby-throated hummingbirds spend their time in these warm places where the other hummingbirds live. But in the springtime they fly North again to visit our northern flowers and to make their tiny nests.

THE BIGGEST BIRD

The biggest bird may grow to be about eight feet tall. Its name is *ostrich*. Once great numbers of wild ostriches lived in sandy deserts in Africa. Nowadays there are not so many wild ones, but tame ones live on ostrich farms.

The reason people keep ostriches on farms is that

these giant birds have beautiful feathers, called plumes, on their wings. The plumes are cut off once a year and sold. These birds cannot fly, because their wings are small and weak; but they can run as swiftly as horses. Men found that it was much easier to care for ostriches on farms than it was to try to catch the wild ones.

When it is time to take the feathers from an ostrich, the great bird is put into a three-cornered pen. The men stand behind him while they cut off the plumes. It would not do to get in front of an ostrich, because he can kick in front and hurt people. But he cannot kick anyone who stands behind him. A hood shaped something like a stocking is slipped over the head of the ostrich and then he stands quietly. It does not hurt the bird to have his feathers snipped off.

Women who like to wear feathers on their hats can wear ostrich plumes (or ornaments made from ostrich feathers) without doing any wrong. It is right to wear feathers that come from birds that are not killed or hurt for the sake of their feathers. People who keep ostriches are kind to them. There is nothing cruel in the way their plumes are taken from them.

Feathers

Perhaps you would like to take a feather and look to see what sort of parts it has and how these parts fit together. A feather is more interesting than you may think. You could really have a very pleasant time looking

165

carefully at one. I think you do not need to be told that birds are the only animals on which feathers grow.

Do you know some of the uses which people have for the feathers of hens and geese and ducks?

Do you know some of the reasons why there are laws in the United States against using the feathers of certain wild birds on hats?

Do you know some of the things which boys and girls who belong to Junior Audubon Clubs learn about helping wild birds?

There is, of course, not room enough in one chapter to tell about many kinds of birds. You will learn about a few more in other chapters in this book. But the best place of all to learn about birds is out of doors, where you can watch them fly and build their nests and feed their young, and where you can hear them sing.

A very wise bird, in spite of the fact that it was called a goose.

THE WISE OLD GOOSE

Once when my little cousin Dick
    Was bragging 'bout how he could swim
And float and dive, old Mother Goose
    Said "Hiss-s-s-s!" and looked at him.

And then Dick sort of hung his head
    And walked 'way from the shady pool,
'Cause Mother Goose had all her flock
    Out swimming where 'twas nice and cool.

And they could stretch and flap their wings,
    And reach their heads way under, deep,
And row about with paddle feet!
    They even floated in their sleep!

To see the little goslings play,
    Who didn't need to learn to swim,
Made boasting Dickie's face turn red
    When Mother Goose said "Hiss-s!" to him.

CHAPTER XI

CAVES AND DUG-OUTS

Did you ever find a hole in the ground and play that it was your secret cave, where you could go when you wished to be quite safe, and where you could put things that you wished to hide?

There are many animals that hide things in the ground, and there are many that live in caves for part or all of their lives. This chapter tells about a few of them.

THE HOME OF AN EARTHWORM

Probably you can find the burrow of an *earthworm* (or *angleworm*) if you hunt in places where the ground is not too dry. The robins know where to hunt. If you cannot find one without help, watch a robin some morning and let him show you where "the early bird catches the worm." When you have caught your earthworm, you can keep it alive in a flowerpot filled with earth, and learn to know a very interesting little footless animal.

An earthworm comes up out of its burrow at night

to seek food. Sometimes all it needs to do is to stretch its head end out of the hole and eat what it finds within reach. Sometimes food may not be so near, and then the little animal needs to come out to find it. The worm will eat leaves that are growing near the ground and old, partly decayed leaves. It likes meat, too, and seeks broken parts of insects or other meaty bits.

It seems strange that a little earless, eyeless, footless earthworm can do so many things.

When daylight comes, the worm slips into a burrow, but it stays near the top of the hole in the morning until the ground has been warmed by the sun. The early bird finds it there within reach and, by grabbing quickly and pulling firmly, tugs it out of the hole. Can you tell, by watching a robin, whether the bird sees the worm or hears it?

If you put your ear to the ground in a place where many earthworms live, can you hear them moving about? Some people say they can.

An earthworm has no paws with which to dig. It has no rooting snout. Its body is very soft. How then can it dig a hole in the hard ground? It digs by eating its way into the ground. It swallows the dirt, and very often it takes in a mouthful of vegetable or animal stuff that serves for food. But whether or not there is food in the soil, the worm swallows it. The soil is then passed through its body and pushed out on top of the ground in the shape of little pellets called *castings*. After a worm has swallowed earth, it soon comes to the surface to empty its body. It pushes out its tail, which it uses like a little trowel in placing the castings first on one side and then on another. If a worm finds a crack underground, it sometimes pokes its castings into that, instead of coming to the surface.

The two ends of an earthworm look so much alike that you will need to look closely to tell which is which. As this animal can crawl backward as well as forward, you cannot find out which is the head by watching one move about. There are other queer things about this strange creature. It breathes through its skin. It has no eyes, but the head end of its body is sensitive to light. It does not mind a little light for a short time, so it can be watched by lantern light or with a flash light; but an earthworm returns to its burrow before bright daylight. That is, a well one does. Sometimes you may find sick worms on top of the ground in the daytime.

An earthworm has no ears and does not hear sounds as do animals with ears. Once a man tooted whistles and pounded on a piano to see if he could scare an earthworm into its hole with loud sounds. He found that a worm is not frightened by noises. But its body can feel the least jarring of the ground, and you will need to walk very carefully if you find one before it crawls into its burrow. An earthworm can feel, too, the slightest touch on its skin—even the breeze of your breath will make it go into its hole for safety.

This little earless and eyeless and footless animal can do other things, too, besides digging a burrow and finding its food. It can plug the top of its burrow with leaves, so that it is like a tube with a cork in it. When the worm does this, it drags the leaves into the top of the burrow, small end first, and pulls in enough to fill the opening. You may have seen little bunches of leaves standing up in holes in the ground, without guessing how they came there.

When the ground is warm enough and moist enough near the surface, earthworms live only a few inches from the top of the ground. When it is too dry there, they sink their burrows deeper and deeper to find what moisture they need. When the cold days of autumn come, they dig deep enough to be below frost. They put into their burrows tiny stones or hard seeds, on which they rest. Some people think the worms can breathe better that way. The air around the little round things in their beds touches the worms underneath, so there is air below as well as above. Their winter caves are made bigger than the size of the hole at the top of the ground, and sometimes several worms roll themselves up into a little ball and sleep together on the same bed of pebbles. There they rest, safe from the frost and wintry weather, until spring wakens them to their active life of digging.

Did you ever think what so many tunnels, here, there, and everywhere, do to the ground? The earthworms really keep the ground stirred and changed as if they were little plows working busily all summer. The earthworms help wild plants to grow in one of the ways that people help garden plants—by stirring the soil near their roots.

THE DEN OF A BUMBLEBEE

Perhaps you have been thinking that a bumblebee lives only among flowers, where she hums happy-sounding tunes with her wings. She does spend a great many hours among blossoms, to be sure. It is well for the plants that she does, for she carries pollen from flower to flower as she visits first one and then another.

A pollen grain, as you may know, has in it the bit of life that a plant must have to help it form a living seed. Pollen grows in one part of a blossom and it must be scattered on another part of the blossom before it can reach the seed cell. Pollen is scattered in several different ways. Two of the ways are by wind and by insects.

The bumblebee is one of the insects that help plants to grow seeds by carrying pollen for them. Red clover, indeed, has no other way of growing enough seeds. The wind cannot get at its pollen to scatter it. The tube of this blossom is too deep and slender for most pollen-carrying insects. But the bumblebee has mouth parts that reach into the slender tube far enough to touch the pollen.

The bumblebee does not know that it is helping the clover. It is attracted by the sweet nectar at the bottom of the long clover tube. If you pull one of these tubes out of a head of clover blossoms and suck the tip of it, you can tell how sweet a drink the bumblebee finds.

You may see the bumblebee among red clovers and other flowers so much that you think she lives in such places all the time. But she does not. Her home is in another place altogether, for she is a cave dweller.

In the spring a queen bumblebee hunts for a nice dry little den in the ground where she can make a home.

Do you live where you can take a walk across the field or along the edge of the woods? If you do, go out next spring quite early, as soon as the snow is gone; or perhaps even before it is all gone in the shadiest hollow in the woods. If you cannot do this next spring, make up your mind that you will some spring, even if you need to wait until you are forty years old.

It is a walk worth taking, because you may meet a bumblebee queen. She will be dressed in black with yellow trimmings, furry-looking or velvety. She will be flying very slowly as if hunting for something—and so she will be! She will be flying very low as if what she seeks is in the ground—and so it is!

The queen bumblebee will be humming a tune with her wings. It will not be a loud, gay tune such as you have heard a bumblebee sing in the summer when she was filling her pollen baskets in a wild rose or filling her honey sac with nectar from a clover. It will be a low tune—her house-hunting song, and it is springtime music. When you hear it, you will know it for the song of a queen bumblebee seeking a den where she can find shelter and where she can hide her treasure.

You know that different people like different kinds of houses. Animals, also, choose different kinds of homes. Some cave dwellers live in damp dens, as the earthworm does. Some prefer dry ones. Some like them in the shade. Some would rather have them in sunny places.

It so happens that the bumblebee and the field mouse like exactly the same sort of cave. This is very pleasant for the bumblebee; for all she needs, when she goes house-hunting, is to find a vacant den that a field mouse has left. That is what suits her best of all. She may have to do a little house cleaning, but the chances are that the furniture suits her very well as it is. The nest of dry grass that the field mouse made is good enough for her use.

When the bumblebee has chosen her den, she gathers some pollen and a little nectar from spring flowers. With this she makes her first loaf of beebread. She does not eat it herself, but places it in the nest in her den and lays a few eggs on the loaf.

She broods her eggs like a mother bird, covering them over with her body. Of course, as she has no warm, red blood, her body is not warm like that of a bird. But her fuzzy body keeps the cold air from touching her eggs and helps them to hatch. Some wax oozes out of the wax glands opening on the under side of her body. She brushes this off and makes a cup of it near her eggs. While the sun is shining she fills this cup with honey, which she sips when the weather is too cold for her to leave her eggs.

When the eggs hatch, the soft, white, little babies, without fuzz or wings or feet, are so hungry that their mother must fetch much pollen and nectar to mix for their food. The bee babies grow big and fat and then they rest in their cocoons. While they are waiting in their cocoons each one changes from a hairless, footless, wingless thing to a grown bee with four wings and six legs and a velvet gown of black and yellow fuzz.

Since the queen bumblebee lays a great many eggs, her grown daughters find much work to do to take care of their baby sisters. I think they like working. I think so because they always have a happy-sounding hum as they go searching for pollen and nectar, and they are pleasant to one another at home.

I never heard a cross note from bumblebees unless they were frightened or abused in some way or their home was in danger. Then they can make angry sounds with their wings and use sharp stings. I know that they can stand up for their rights. Twice bumblebees have stung me. When I was about three years old I smelled a blossom that had a bumblebee in it. That one stung my nose, and my mother thought that I looked more like a little pig with a long snout than a child. The bee was not to be blamed. I had frightened it. The second time was not many years ago. I rolled under a fence just where there happened to be a bumblebee den. On the way home I met some friends who did not know who I was, because I looked so queer. Those bees were not to be blamed, either. That was the only way they had of teaching me not to come blundering so suddenly and roughly at the door of their den. There is nothing mean about bumblebees, but it is a very bad plan to frighten them.

All the children of the queen bumblebee are workers until late in the summer, when there are some different kinds of children that grow up in the den. Some of these different ones are sons who go by the name of *drones*, and some of them are daughters who are called young queens. Neither the drones nor the young queens do any work in their mother's home. There are so many workers late in the summer that their help is not needed.

The young queen must save her strength until springtime. There will be work enough for her to do then. She sips what nectar she needs from flowers and she helps herself from the honey she finds in the den. After a while she takes a nap. It is a long nap. It lasts from August until April or May.

When she is ready to take her winter's nap, she goes away quite by herself. She finds a place that suits her needs (a sandy well-drained bank will do), and there she digs a tiny den. On the sandy floor of that wee bedroom she lies, dozy and quiet, a little sleeping beauty waiting for the kiss of the spring to waken her and send her humming on her way while she hunts a bigger den in which to bring up her family.

Once there was a bee—a bumblebee
Who slept 'til spring had come.
When the winter broke, she then awoke
And her wings began to hum.

THE PAINTED TURTLE'S HIDDEN TREASURE

You might not guess that a turtle has a treasure to hide. She paddles about in the pond as contentedly as if paddling during a hot summer day is the only joy needed in her life. Or when she is not paddling, she is resting on a pleasant island of stone, quite ready for a dive, just as you see her in the picture on the cover of this book. Or, if she is hungry, she has a good time hunting. She reaches her head out of the water, looking and listening to be sure that all is safe and quiet; and then she puts her head down and pokes about here and

When an ant-lion is young, it is a queer little creature with tong-shaped jaws. It makes a pit with smooth sloping seeds and lives hidden in a hole at the bottom. When grown up, it has wings and flies away. If you find such pits in the sand, watch to see what tumbles into them.

there catching bits of food. If she catches a piece too big to swallow at a gulp, she carves her meat in a comical way. She holds it firmly in her mouth and then pushes it first with one front foot and then with the other, one on each side, until it is torn smaller and smaller and is at last of a size to be swallowed easily. What with her paddling and her resting and her hunting, it hardly seems that a turtle can have any hidden treasure on her mind.

Perhaps she has forgotten it. But in June she left her pond and took a walk on the sandy shore. There she dug a hole in the sand with her paddling feet, which serve almost as well for scooping spades as they do for oars. Then she laid her eggs in the hole. After tucking them in with a cover of sand, she left them to the warmth of the sun. You can feel that the sun could brood her eggs, if you will put your hand into sand which is heated by the sun.

Whether she forgot all about her nest I cannot say. Whether or not she forgot, it is certain that every June since she was old enough she has hidden treasures in a nest dug in the sand. And every June, as long as she can, she will dig in just that way. There will be many Junes for her, if all goes well, for turtles live many years if they are not harmed.

And who would be so horrid as to harm a painted turtle? No one who has seen the pretty bright red and yellow trimming on her dark shell. No one who has found the mother turtle at her nest in the sand. No one who has watched the baby turtles take their first walk from the nest to the pond where they can swim and dive.

The Hole of a Bank Swallow

Years ago I used to play near the banks of the Mississippi River. There were many wonderful things to watch there, both plants and animals.

One day when I looked up at a high place in a steep bank, I saw some small round holes leading into the side of the bank. I climbed up to the lowest one and put in my arm as far as it would reach. The tips of my fingers touched something soft and warm. I had found some little birds that were not yet old enough to fly, some young *bank swallows*.

Bank swallows are smaller than the tree swallows that live in bird boxes. Their backs are mouse-colored and their throats are white. They are pretty to watch and I am glad that they live in many parts of the country. It may be that you will find a bank where they are digging their holes with their little bills. Perhaps you will see them dipping down to the top of some water and taking a bath as they fly.

If you watch bank swallows, you will be sure to see them catching flies or little grasshoppers or other insects that trouble people. All kinds of swallows catch such insects. When they are hunting they fly back and forth in the air, sometimes high and sometimes low.

THE CRICKET'S CAVE

One day when I was writing this chapter, I stopped long enough to take a walk. I thought I would try to find a *cricket's* cave to tell you about.

The leaves on the maple trees were red and yellow; and I think you can guess what time of year it was. As I walked near the edge of a field, I heard some music. It was music made with wings. It was not the humming tune of bees. It was the tune that Mr. Cricket makes.

I went quietly toward the spot where the music seemed to be, but I found no cricket there. By that time the music seemed to be coming from quite another direction. So I went here and there and back again until at last I saw a little black musician standing at the doorway of his cave. His wings were lifted a little and when he scraped one against the other he made a pleasant sound.

As long as I stood still, he kept on with his tune. The sun was very bright and after a time I put up my hand to shade my eyes. The shadow of my moving hand fell across the little musician, and Mr. Cricket slipped quickly into his cave. His doorway was between two small stones. Inside there was a narrow tunnel where he hid.

Not many steps away I met Mrs. Cricket. There was no music in her wings. She could not spend the bright fall days making tunes. She had other things to do. When I saw her, she was standing on an old ant hill

181

Mrs. Cricket made a hole in the ground with the long needle-shaped tool she wears at the end of her body. Then she laid some eggs. Now she is patting the ground smooth over the egg-hole.

where the ground was soft and dry. At the tip of her body was a long slender thing that looked like a black needle. That was the tool she used when she laid her eggs. She thrust it into the soft ground and left some eggs hidden there. Then she raked the place with her jaws and patted it until there was no mark to show where her eggs were hidden. Just then I came too near and Mrs. Cricket ran into a little hole between two stems of grass. Her cave was a narrow tunnel like that of Mr. Cricket.

After that I came away and I suppose that Mr. Cricket came out of his cave and went on with his tune, and that Mrs. Cricket came out of hers and went on with her egg-laying.

THE WOODCHUCK'S TUNNEL

A railroad train goes into one end of a tunnel and out at the other. That is what a *woodchuck* can do. He does not need to come out the way he goes in, unless he wishes. He has a front door where the loose dirt from his cave is heaped in a mound. He has back doors that are holes without any mounds, and more than likely those back doors are hidden where no one but the woodchuck finds them.

The woodchuck I knew best of all had his back doorway under a stone pile. I never saw the doorway; but I used to see Billy (that was the name I gave him, and he did not mind) standing beside the stone pile when I sat in the fence corner not far away. He would stand up on his hind legs and drop his front paws. It was not a trick that I taught him. It was a pretty habit of his own.

Sometimes, while he stood there, he would whistle a clear, musical little tune. No one taught him that, either, unless he learned it from his mother or father.

Billy had other tricks, too, and he did them all perfectly. One was his "freezing" trick. He might be playing about the stone pile or climbing a rail fence when I came near enough to startle him. Then he would "freeze"—that is, he would keep as still as a frozen woodchuck until I went on. That was his way of hiding in plain sight. It was a good way, because foxes and dogs would not chase him if they did not see him; and who can see a motionless woodchuck on a brown-gray stone or a gray-brown rail?

He had another way of hiding that I liked, so sometimes I went to call on Billy at his front door. That was far out in the clover field, so his tunnel must have been a long one. I could never get near his doorway without his knowing. Even if I went so quietly that he did not hear me, a crow would be sure to see me and tell. Of course the crow did not say, in so many words, "Here comes a person!" but he called out "Caw" in a tone that all the crows within hearing and all the woodchucks in the field understood.

When the crow called "Caw" in his warning tone, Billy would run to his doorway and then stand up on his hind legs so that he could see above the tall grass and clover. Then he would perform his vanishing trick. Probably if I had started toward him, he would have chucked himself into his hole in a hurry. But I would stand still—as still as I was able, although I could not "freeze" as well as he could. And while I waited there, Billy would sink down little by little until after a while he was not standing up. Then, so slowly that I could hardly see a motion, he would slip into his hole, hind legs first, and then go down and down, hardly more than a hair at a time, until only his head would be out and then at last even that would seem to fade away.

One day in spring when I met Billy, I noticed that he looked queer. He looked as if he had been growing some huge whiskers, which stuck out at each side of his mouth. When he came nearer I could see that he was

Two woodchucks (marmots) that live in Yellowstone National Park.

carrying wisps of dry grass. He was not whistling (I suppose that he could not with his mouth full of hay), but I thought he seemed cheerful. He took his hay into his front door and down into his tunnel. The hay was not to eat. It was for a nest for Mrs. Chuck and the babies.

Billy did not care for dry food. He liked juicy things such as tender clover heads. He liked wild vegetables;

and if people planted a garden near by, he liked cultivated vegetables, too. He was not very particular which kind of plants he ate if they were tender and juicy, for his appetite was good during three seasons of the year. In the spring he was hungry because he was thin, having eaten nothing all winter. In the summer he was hungry just because he was well and hearty. And in the fall he ate enough to last him all winter.

Different animals prepare for winter in different ways. Most birds fly to warm places where food is not frozen or covered with snow. Squirrels gather a harvest of nuts or other seeds. Each animal does what is best for its body. Billy Woodchuck's way was to put his fall harvest inside of his skin in the form of fat. So he ate until he was fat. Then he ate until he was fatter. Then he kept on eating until he could hardly swallow. After that he went into his tunnel and slept in his nest, down deep enough so that the frost did not reach him. He slept for four or five months until his fat was gone and he was hungry again. By that time it was spring and there were fresh juicy things beginning to grow. He was so glad that he whistled.

CHAPTER XII

BUILDINGS OF STONE AND OTHER EARTHY STUFFS

There are many animals, not living in caves, that build dwellings of earthy materials they get on or in the ground. You may like to see if you can think of other animals that do this besides those you read about in this chapter.

THE STONE HUT OF A WATER BABY

You may not expect a young creature to make a stone dwelling in which to live; but when I tell you that the youngster is an insect, you need not be surprised at anything it does. You know that the young of some insects (such as honeybees and bumblebees) are quite helpless and need to be fed; but a young *caddis* can take care of itself very well, as you shall see.

The best way to see is to look for yourself. The shallow edge of a pond or a stream is the place where a young caddis may be found. When you lie down on a log or low plank bridge or a flat rock and look down into the shallow water, keeping quiet so that you will not disturb anything, you will see queer little things moving about. The things seem to be made of stones or bits of sticks or rubbish, and so they are.

Such moving bundles of sticks and tubes of stones are interesting things to have at school or at home, if they are kept in plenty of fresh water. Each one has a young caddis inside. It is a very good game to see how many different kinds of caddis cases you can find.

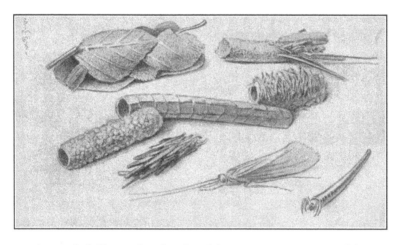

Several different kinds of caddis cases. A young caddis has its head and legs out of the end of the small case at the right. Near it is a grown caddis resting, with its wings held close to its body.

If you choose to find stone cases, you must hunt where the bed of the stream or pond is pebbly or sandy. Did you ever see a stained-glass window which is made of many small pieces of glass of different shapes fitted together into one big window? There is a kind of caddis that takes little clear pebbles and glues them together so that they fit as well as the pieces in a stained-glass window. This sort of case is less than an inch long, and the pebbles used in it are very tiny indeed.

The young caddis does all its building under water. Where do you suppose it gets its glue? There are some glands in the body of the caddis where the glue is made. This is pressed out through openings near the mouth of the caddis and used for sticking together the tiny pebbles. It is a kind of glue that stays waterproof after it hardens. It is something like the silk that caterpillars use, and it comes out of the same sort of glands.

The young caddis looks something like a caterpillar, as you can see when it sticks its head end out of the opening in the case; but the six legs near its head are longer than those of a caterpillar. The second and third pairs of legs are used for creeping along the bottom of the pond and for clinging to the stems of water plants. The front legs are used as hands at mealtime, and they help like hands when the caddis is putting new pieces on the edge of its case with its mouth.

The case is not grown to the body of a caddis as a shell is to the body of a snail, but it is held in place by hooks on the tail of the caddis. When the caddis needs to hide from a hungry fish, it can slip backward into its case and then what fish can see that there is anything there except a few pebbles or sticks?

At last the time comes when the caddis is a water baby no longer. It is time for it to leave its hut and seek the air. It climbs a stem and molts its skin and flies away—for it is now a grown insect with wings.

The grown caddis is a little night creature; and like

many other night animals, it is attracted by lights. It really should fly by the light of the moon. That is what such insects did in the old times before there were electric lights or lamps or candles. But now that there are so many things giving light, some of these little creatures of moonlight go headlong toward electric lights or fires because they cannot tell the difference. You may have seen a caddis trying to get through the window some night when there were lights inside your house. It is grayish or brownish and it looks something like a gray or brown moth when it is flying. When it is resting, it holds its wings sloping down from the sides of its body like the sides of a roof.

It is pleasant to watch for the insects that come to the windows of lighted rooms at night. If you do this some summer you may meet many interesting little creatures that are tapping at your window to get in.

While you are thinking about insects that fly toward light at night, do not forget the *fireflies*. These insects are little beetles. They do not need to come to our windows, as they have lights of their own. Each firefly carries a light at the end of its body. Of course it cannot fly toward that because it cannot fly backward, but it can fly toward the lights of other little fireflies. That is what it does, and that seems to be why fireflies go in flocks at night. They make light for one another. You may see a flock of fireflies in summer flying near a marsh. It will do you no harm if you run and catch one, and if you are gentle it will do the firefly no harm. You can put it under a glass in a dark room and watch it. You can touch the light and not be burned, for it is cool. You can see that it is the end of the body itself that is light. Then you can take the firefly out of doors and let it go its own way to find the flock of lights near the marsh.

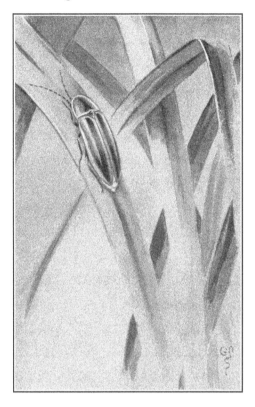

A firefly at rest. It carries a light in the end of its body.

THE ROOM THAT A MASON WASP BUILDS

There dwells a potter in Insect Land,
    A skillful potter she,—
Although she hasn't any hand,
    Her jug is fair to see.

You might be surprised to find a little clay jug sitting on a willow branch, for what can a pretty clay jug be doing on a willow twig?

Before you are over your surprise, a queer little creature alights on the branch near the jug. She has a very, very slender, pinched-looking waist; but you must not blame her for that, because she is a kind of wasp and grows that way naturally.

She walks with a restless shake of her wings to the open jug and drops in something that she brought in her mouth.

"Is it your jug?" you ask her, "and what did you put into it?"

Who put a little clay jug on a willow twig?

The queer little wasp answers never a word. She walks along the branch with a jerky flirt of her wings and flies away without even noticing you.

Before long she is back again, and this time you look sharply and quickly and see that it is a little green caterpillar that she drops into the jug. The caterpillar is limp and it does not squirm. It does not crawl out of the jug while the wasp is away hunting for more. She brings another and another and another, until the jug is full of limp caterpillars.

The next time the wasp comes she has something different in her mouth. It is a ball of clay, and with it she plugs the mouth of the jug very smoothly and nicely. The little potter has now finished the jug that she made and filled and sealed without any help. She will not come back to it again.

It will do no harm if you cut off the branch carefully and take it home, jug and all.

The mother wasp has no need of her finished jug, but there is something inside that has use for the canned meat that has been packed away. Before she sealed the jug, the mother insect put in an egg. When the egg hatches, the baby wasp will have plenty of food to eat, and there is nothing that would agree with it so well as tiny caterpillars. As this kind of young wasp is a soft, helpless, footless little thing (much like a baby hornet or a bee) it cannot catch food for itself. It does not need to try. There is enough in the jug.

About twelve days later a little hole will be broken in one side of the jug and out will come a queer little slender-waisted creature who lifts her wings with an uneasy jerk when she walks. So you will open the window and set her free; and perhaps you will sing as she flies away:

> There goes a potter of Insect Land,
> A skillful potter she,—
> For though she hasn't any hand,
> Her jug is fair to see.

Clay Tenements of the Eave Swallows

Wasps are not the only masons with wings. The eave swallow builds its home with clay. You may remember that you have already read about two kinds of swallows in this book and that one of them, the bank swallow, digs a home in a steep bank. The *eave swallow* (or *cliff swallow*) likes a steep place for its home; and though it cannot dig, it does something else that is quite as wonderful. It builds its home on the outside of a cliff instead of inside a bank.

Before white men came to this country and put up high buildings, these swallows used stone cliffs. Now they find that the wall of a barn serves as well—perhaps better, as it has a sheltering eave. There is another reason why swallows like to be near barns. There are usually many flies there for them to eat. Farmers should be very glad to have swallows near by to catch houseflies and horseflies and other troublesome kinds of insects.

An eave swallow might well be called a mason swallow, since it can handle a hod and trowel as well as any mason, and can make a strong good-looking dwelling in a very short time. The hod it uses is its mouth, and it can hold as much as half a thimbleful. I hope some day you may have the fun of seeing one come to the nest it is building. It pushes the clay out of its mouth with its tongue, and it uses the top of its bill like a trowel to put the clay into place at the edge of the nest.

Eave swallows resting near their nest.

Eave swallows seem to know where to get the kind of mud that will make the best houses. They like a place in a moist clay road where the passing wheels have pressed the clay into ruts; or a place near a drinking pool in a pasture where the cows have squeezed the clay with their hoofs. Such mud is firm, yet it is soft and molds into shape like putty.

It is a pretty sight to see one of these birds gather its clay. It does it daintily. It alights on the ground and puts its bill down to make a little ball of the clay; and all the time its wings are held quivering in the air, like those of a butterfly about to take flight.

An eave swallow has chestnut-colored feathers on its throat and the sides of its head, and a pale mark shaped like a new moon on its forehead. Its back is a beautiful steel-blue. When it is building, it gets its pretty face muddy; but afterwards it shakes and rubs its feathers until they are clean again.

Usually a number of these birds build their homes close together. They seem to be happy, for they make pleasant squeaking sounds. They work very busily while they are building; but now and then they take a recess and go hunting for insects in the air over the fields and about the barnyard.

Later, when their clay homes have been finished and furnished with thin, soft beds, and their eggs have been laid and brooded and hatched, then they need to hunt for their young as well as for themselves.

The young birds need an astonishing number of insects before their feathers are grown and they can fly. After they are out of their nests and their wings are strong, there comes a day when they start with the old birds on a hunting trip to the far South, where they stay until spring invites them to take a hunting flight to the North again.

So each spring, with cheerful squeakings, these feathered masons come back to build their homes of clay against a wall of stone or wood. And often so many pairs build on the same wall that their nests are crowded together like tenements in a city.

OTHER EARTH HOMES

Some of the little creatures in this chapter have built their homes of stone and some have used clay. We have called them masons.

Some men are called masons. When masons build, they use different materials from those carpenters use. Do you know what masons build with?

You may like to try to remember how many houses you have seen that masons have built from stuff that is taken out of the ground.

CHAPTER XIII

TRAVELING HOMES

Sometimes you may hear a person say, "My home is wherever I hang up my hat." Perhaps he will say it sadly, as if he wished he had a home where he could keep more than a hat—much more. Perhaps he will say it cheerfully, as if there were no gladder adventure than going from place to place.

A friend of mine lived for many years on a sailing ship at sea; and the far ports of the world seem, to her, neighboring sorts of places where she has stopped now and again to make a call. When I bought the place where I live, she said, "Isn't it a bit too much like dropping anchor for good and all?" To her a home that travels seems better than one that is fastened to the ground.

THE HOME OF THE SNAIL

You have read in other chapters in this book about animals with ten, eight, six, four, and two feet. You have read about animals with no feet at all. But nothing has yet been said about an animal with one foot.

A snail has one foot. It is big and broad and flat—the

whole under side of the snail's body is a foot. A snail is sometimes called a stomach-footed animal because it looks as if it were creeping on its stomach. The foot of the snail is sticky. In fact there is so much stickiness about it that it leaves a trail behind it showing where it passed.

Even when a snail has traveled for hours, it is still at home, for its house is always on its back.

When I was three or four years old, I used to watch snails very often; and I wondered if the snail was hurt and if the sticky trail it left behind was something it was losing out of its body. Once upon a time grown people had the same funny thought about snails. They had an idea that the sticky track made by a snail as it crawled along was lost from the stuff of its body; and that the farther it crept, the smaller it became, until at last there was nothing left of the snail but its track and its shell. Because of this idea they used to speak of "a snail which melteth."

But the snail does not melt. Its body is bigger at the end of its summer's journey than it was at the beginning, although it has left behind it a shiny trail as long as the sum of all its trips added together. The body of the snail makes its "mucilage" as fast as it needs it.

Of course an animal with but one foot would need a special way of traveling. Pushing ahead and sticking as it goes is a sure way of getting somewhere. Sure but slow! If you wish to enjoy watching a snail, you must do it when you feel in no greater hurry than the snail does.

Why should a snail hurry its journey when it never need worry about going back to its starting place? It never needs to *go* home, because it always *is* at home. If a snail goes berrying when berries are ripe and juicy, it can spend the day or the night among the fruit and be in no danger of losing its way. If something suddenly startles the snail, it can make itself safe at home by hiding inside its shell, and that is one thing that this slow creature can do quickly. If, on a warm sunny day, the snail is tired of the heat, it moves in its sticky-footed way into the shade, house and all.

A snail takes comfort in its own home. Its house fits its body better than an easy chair. It keeps the wetness of the rain outside and it keeps the moisture of the snail's body inside. The wind cannot blow through its walls.

It is a thin and pretty house, and always exactly the right size. When the snail first hatches, its house is a tiny one with but a single "turn" in it. As a snail travels and eats and grows until its foot is bigger and broader, the house has more and bigger turns in it so that the dweller and the dwelling fit each other all the time. It is well that they do fit, for they are grown together inside. The snail cannot move out of one shell and into another as a hermit crab can.

The snail does not need another shell. If it should spend all its life poking its eyes into other shells, it could never find one better suited to its needs than the one which grows on its own body.

It may be you think that noses, and not eyes, are what are poked into places. That depends on the animal that does the poking. A snail pokes with its eyes. This queer animal has two eyes, and each one is on the tip of a soft peg which can stretch until it is long or shrink until it is short. The snail can shrink one eye peg and stretch the other at the same time. It can poke one eye over the edge of a leaf without peeping down with the other. It can pull the outside of the peg inside, drawing the eye out of sight in that way.

If you have been amused by the snail's strange way of walking with one sticky foot, and by its queer ways of poking eye pegs, you may be ready to smile at the way a snail can vanish inside its house and fasten the door after itself. If a bird or a person or some other animal comes suddenly near, the snail folds its broad flap of a foot lengthwise and pulls itself into its shell.

Then there is nothing to be seen but a quiet shell

house, across the doorway of which is drawn a snug, smooth shutter held fast as a bolted door.

A Tiny Brown House on a Sweet Fern Leaf

It may be that the sweet fern grows in the part of the country where you live. Sweet fern is not a fern at all, as you may know, but a bush with fragrant leaves shaped somewhat like those of certain ferns. Some people like this spicy scent so well that they use the leaves in pillows.

It is not for a pillow, however, that one small creature uses the leaves. What it wants is food—sweet fern leaf for breakfast, sweet fern leaf for dinner, sweet fern leaf for supper, and sweet fern leaf for all the luncheons between meals. You may think that by the time so greedy a youngster becomes full-fed, there will be no sweet fern leaves on the bushes. But the bushes send up many new sprouts and there are plenty of leaves to spare for the hungry creature who, you must remember, is very small.

This very small animal with a very big appetite lives in a traveling house that looks like a tiny brown shell. This house serves in a shell-like way to protect its owner from weather and enemies. The house and the owner do not grow together as do the snail and its shell. In fact, this house cannot really be said to grow. It becomes bigger and bigger as the traveler grows, but that is because the traveler inside keeps adding more to the edge of the shell. He uses little pellets of soft brown stuff and shapes them with his jaws into the edge of his house. Very likely the moisture from his mouth helps to make the substance glue-like so that it is firm when it dries. The traveler need never carry a house that is too big for him, since he can put on an addition at the doorway at any time. The tiny brown house on the sweet fern bush does not go on a one-footed journey like the house of the snail. There are six little feet that stick out of the doorway to drag the house along. A little head sticks out, too, to eat as many mouthfuls of sweet fern as the traveler wants.

The brown house and the beetle under the sweet fern are shaped like their pictures, but they are much smaller.

The six legs and the head belong to a young beetle

who has not yet grown old enough to have wings. After a time the young insect becomes too sleepy to eat another bite of sweet fern. He takes a strange sort of nap and when he wakens he is a fully grown beetle quite different from the little creature who went to sleep. He now has a hard covering on his body and no longer needs a shell-like house to protect him.

When I tell you that this fully grown beetle is still so small that it would take six like him, going single file, to reach an inch, you can see why you might need to look carefully at the sweet fern bush to find him at all.

He is so small, indeed, that you may wish to pick him up to see how he looks. When you try to do that, he doubles his legs and folds them close to his body and drops to the ground. He lies there without stirring; and if you find him at all, it will be because you hunt very carefully indeed. That is his way of hiding, and it is a very good way, when a bird happens to come near enough to shake the bush.

The next time you try to catch such a beetle, you will put your hand under him and let him drop into that. Then you will have a chance to see what a queer little fellow he really is. His back is covered with little humps, and he looks more like a tiny bronze ornament than he does like a live thing.

At least he does not look alive until he unfolds his six legs and starts to walk away.

The Larch Case Bearer

Do you know what sort of tree the American larch is? (Some people call it a hackmatack and some call it a tamarack.) This tree belongs to the same family as the pine tree. Its leaves are short and slender and they grow in little tufts. The larch tree does not keep its leaves all winter as most members of the Pine Family do. But, like its relatives, it has cones. The larch cones are a pretty rosy color while they are growing. When they are a little more than half an inch long, they stop growing and turn brown. Inside the brown cone are seeds, each with a flat wing.

A twig from a larch tree, with some case bearers at the left and a moth at the right. (The case bearer that lives on apple trees changes into a moth with fringed wings much like the wings of the moth in the picture.)

On this interesting kind of tree there often lives a caterpillar so tiny that it can hide inside the slender needle-shaped larch leaf. First it nibbles a round hole into the leaf and sticks in its head. Then it eats as far as it can reach and creeps in as far as it eats, until after a little while it is all inside the leaf and the green stuff that was in the leaf is inside the caterpillar. The tiny caterpillar now cuts the slender tight-fitting leaf off the tree and marches along the twig with the leaf-tube for its house. There is room at the cut-off end to reach out its feet so that it can walk, and to stretch out its head so that it can eat.

The caterpillar lives in this house all winter, though it spins a little silk to make the tiny room quite snug during the long nap. After the green leaves of the larch have faded and fallen, the queer little dwelling stays on the twig, where the winter winds blow on it and the zero days chill it. Though it is so tiny and frail, the caterpillar lives through the cold and wakens in the spring hungrier than ever.

After it has eaten a long spring breakfast, the caterpillar finds its house too narrow. So it splits the thin wall along the side and puts in a strip from another dried larch leaf, mending the place nicely with silk threads which come out of silk glands near its mouth.

When it has eaten enough to be a full-fed caterpillar, it spins some more silk for a cocoon, inside of which it changes from a caterpillar to a tiny moth with fringes on its wings.

A Case Bearer on an Apple Tree

The apple tree belongs to the Rose Family. If you live near an apple tree, you may like to see in what ways an apple blossom is like a wild rose blossom. If you cannot find an apple tree, perhaps you can find a cherry tree or a plum tree or a peach tree or a raspberry bush or a blackberry bush or a strawberry plant. They all belong to the Rose Family, and it is interesting to see in what ways the blossoms of any two of them are alike.

It is not apple blossoms that a certain little caterpillar likes. It likes apple leaves, and it has a queer way of eating them. It has other queer ways, too. When it hatches out of the egg its mother moth laid, it has not any house at all. At first it bites a hole through one layer of an apple leaf and begins to eat some of the stuff inside the leaf. As it eats it pushes its head in farther and farther to reach another mouthful, until after a little while the caterpillar (now a *leaf miner*) is all inside the leaf living in the tunnel it has made by eating.

A tunnel in a leaf is a good enough summer home, but what will happen to the caterpillar when the leaf with the tunnel in it drops down to the ground in the fall? By that time the caterpillar is not in the tunnel. This is how it happens. With its jaws the caterpillar cuts a little curved house out of the apple leaf and fastens the parts together with silk. Then the little traveler puts its feet out through the doorway of its curved house and goes on a journey to a steady branch which will not drop when frosty weather comes. At the end of this trip the caterpillar presses some silk out of its silk glands and makes its shelter snug for the winter.

In the spring, the caterpillar is hungry after fasting for so many months. As the new leaves are tender and tempting, the spring breakfast proves to be a hearty one. After that the curved house seems too small, and then the little traveler moves out and makes one of an altogether different shape.

The new house is made of strips of leaf and silk. It is so straight and narrow that people call its owner the "cigar case bearer." They mean by this name that the case is shaped like a cigar. They do not mean that the house is as large as a cigar. Indeed, the cigar-shaped house is very small to fit the needs of a caterpillar that is about one-fifth of an inch long. After the caterpillar has grown to be as long as that, it spins a silken cocoon inside of which it changes to a little gray moth. When its wings are spread, this moth is not quite half an inch across. These tiny wings have fringed edges that help the moth float in the air when it flies.

You have come to the end of the chapter about traveling houses, but you must not think there are no other kinds than those mentioned in these few pages. There are so many different ones moving from place to place on leaves and twigs that you are likely to meet some of them in a city park or in the country. Some of the most interesting ones I have left for you to find yourself when you go out to hunt for them some day.

CHAPTER XIV

HOUSES OF WOOD

The Cabin of the Common Tree Frog

This is the story of a tree frog (or tree toad) who likes a hollow in an old tree. He likes it well enough to stay near the same one, day after day and week after week. He likes it well enough, indeed, to be there summer after summer, if nothing happens to prevent. And, if the floor of the hollow is soft and moist enough to dig into with little frog fingers, he likes it well enough to bury himself there when he is ready to take his winter's nap.

One name of this tree frog is Hyla, which is rather a pleasing name, I think. It sounds like music. This is as it should be, for Hyla is a musician. His tune is a trill that is somewhat like the purr of a happy cat, though it is loud and it can be heard far away. He sings with his mouth shut and his throat puffed out so that it looks like a toy balloon full of air. His song is for evening or for cloudy days, and it is a pleasant sound to hear.

Many people have heard Hyla's music who have never seen the musician. This is not because he is far away, but because he has a trick of hiding. In his hole?

Hyla, the tree frog, at the door of his cabin.

He is often there, but he does not need to depend on holes as he can hide even while he is in plain sight.

Did it ever happen that one day, when you were sitting on a branch in an apple tree, you put your hand on a gray spot on the bark? The gray spot was cold and it slipped out from under your fingers and jumped. Perhaps you jumped, too, for you were surprised. It may be that you saw which way the gray spot went and yet lost sight of it when it reached the trunk of the tree. What seemed like a piece of jumping bark was Hyla, the tree frog.

The next time you meet Hyla, he may be a green spot on a green leaf, and you may not really know what your eyes are looking at. The next time after that, you may mistake the tree frog for a lump of putty on a white post or a brown spot on a brown fence.

If you happen to see Hyla when he is moving about, however, it will be easy for you to catch him. If you are careful, it will do him no harm for you to keep him some day long enough to watch him change his color. You will see that he does not do this with a powder puff or paint. All he does is to sit still and wait, and after a while his color is changed. His skin cannot turn from green to gray all in a minute. You may sometimes need to watch an hour before Hyla will look so much like what he is sitting on that you lose sight of him. But what is an hour to a tree frog? He is willing to rest all day; and when evening comes, it does not matter so much what color he is.

Hyla's eyes are bright enough in the dusk to see a

moving insect a foot or more away. He is so quick that he can leap from one leaf and catch the insect before he reaches another. He does not care where he lands, because there is always a twig or a leaf or something against which he can fall. He can cling to anything he touches with a hand or foot, because the tips of his fingers and toes are sticky. He can even climb things as smooth as glass.

When Hyla is two inches long, he is a full-sized tree frog. He has an appetite for caterpillars and flies and beetles and some other insects.

When he was younger and only a little more than half an inch long, he liked to eat tiny aphids filled with sweet sap. When he was as little as that he was green— green as the rushes that grow near water.

I saw some Hylas, once, when they were little like that. They were sitting on the flat narrow leaves of rushes that were growing in a lake in Minnesota. They were so tiny that though four or five perched close together, their weight was not enough to bend the thin leaf. They were the color of rushes, and perhaps I should not have seen them if they had kept still. But they leaped and clung to the leaves of the rushes and swayed with them; so by looking all about I could tell that there were hundreds and hundreds of them, maybe a thousand.

It was the time of day when the sun itself could not yet be seen, but there were lovely colors in the sky in the east. Some of the colors showed in the water near the tall rushes with slender leaves that swayed until their tips hung down. Among these graceful leaves, the tiny Hylas were playing, springing here and there and swinging by their tiny hands, or resting in rows on their green perches. Those wee sprites had not found the trees whose branches they would climb later. They were not ready each to seek his own hollow in some old tree. They were just through with being tadpoles in the water and had not yet left the water plants.

Every year, about the time that apple trees blossom, all the old tree frogs within reach of lake or pond or pool take to water. Trees are forgotten for a while, and ponds are remembered. The hands and feet of tree frogs are made for swimming as well as for climbing, and life in the water is pleasant for them in the springtime.

This is the season of the famous Hyla concerts, when every little musician puffs out the song-balloon in his throat and trills and trills.

After the concert season is over, all the old tree frogs travel back to their tree homes, each one alone. But the mothers do not go before they have stuck their eggs to the stems of water plants. The tadpoles that hatch from these eggs grow to be very beautiful, with the color of gold showing in their shiny bodies and the color of flame in their gleaming eyes.

The concert singer in the spring, the darting tadpole in the pool, the tiny acrobat taking exercise among the rushes at sunrise, the soloist purring on a cloudy day, the nimble hunter leaping for his supper at dusk, the spot of changing color, the buried life sleeping through the winter in the hollow cabin—thinking of all the common tree frog is and can do, nobody who lives in

Hyla Land need wish to move into a more interesting country.

(There is a pretty little lizard, common in some southern parts of the United States, that changes its color to green or brown or gray or yellow. This lizard grows to be five or six inches long. It makes an interesting pet. Of course if you catch one, you will let it go again or else you will take good care of it. It will eat flies and some other soft insects and bits of raw meat. It should have water often, but not in a dish. It is in the habit of drinking dewdrops and raindrops from leaves, and it does not know about water in dishes. A pet lizard of this kind needs to have water sprinkled where it can lap the drops. It is a graceful and active little creature and its color changes are wonderful to watch. In some countries, there are other larger lizards that can also change their colors.)

AN EIGHT-STORY APARTMENT
OF A LEAF-CUTTER BEE

There is a little bee, much smaller than a bumblebee and not so downy, that is called a *leaf-cutter*. I once knew one named "Meg" for short, who made an eight-story apartment. Sometimes leaf-cutters make more and sometimes fewer apartments, depending somewhat on the location.

Meg hollowed out a rather soft place in a post until she had a tunnel about four inches long. Then she flew to a rosebush and cut pieces out of the leaves. With these pieces she made a thimble-shaped room that fitted the bottom of the tunnel. Part of the pieces she cut were longer than they were wide, and these she used for the floor and walls of the room. Next she filled the room with pollen moistened with honey, and on this pasty food she placed an egg. She then went back to the rosebush and snipped out some circles as evenly as if her jaws had been cooky cutters. With the circles she made a tight-fitting ceiling. Then she built another thimble-shaped room on top of the first, and continued to build until she had an eight-story apartment. Each room had one egg in it, and enough food of pollen-and-honey paste for what hatched out of the egg.

A piece of old post, split open to show the thimble-shaped nests of a leaf-cutter bee.

Of course Meg's babies hatched out of her eggs, and of course Meg's babies did not look at all like their mother. Baby insects never do look like grown-up insects. Meg's babies were white, footless, wingless, soft little things that looked much like the babies of bumblebees and honeybees and wasps. (Bees and wasps are relatives of Meg's.)

Each one of Meg's babies had a room to itself, where it ate and rested and grew and changed its skin several times. Each room was a nursery, a dining room, and a living room, all in one. When at last they all came out of their rooms, they were babies no longer but grown insects with legs and wings, and they looked like Meg.

Whenever you find a rosebush (and sometimes other kinds of bushes, too) the leaves of which look as if they had been cut with tiny cooky-cutters, you may know that somewhere, not far away, a little bee has hidden her apartments in some tunnel.

THE FLICKER'S NEST

So fond are we all of the gay Yellow-hammer
    That names by the hundred we heap on his head:
The Yar-up, the Wake-up, the Cuckoo Woodpecker,
    And many another before all are said!
Ant-eater, Ant-pecker, High-hole, and High-holder,
    The Gaffer Woodpecker, and Gar-up, I hear,
Are but a beginning of names for the winning
    Gold wing-ed Woodpecker, or Flicker, my dear!

Most of the names that have been given this common and beautiful woodpecker have to do with its colors or flight or the sounds it makes or the habits it has, but some of them are rather silly and do not seem to have much meaning.

Other kinds of woodpeckers eat chiefly insects that they find on or in the trunks and branches of trees. But the flicker is quite as willing to eat grasshoppers and beetles that it finds on the ground as it is to eat tree insects. It likes, too, wild fruit for dessert. The feast which pleases it best, however, is a meal of ants. When a flicker pokes its long bill into an ant hill, the ants

A flicker, like other woodpeckers, uses a hollow in a tree or post for its nest.

rush out to fight. Nothing could suit the hungry flicker better, for this is his chance to dip up the angry little morsels on his sticky tongue with great relish.

Although the flicker is different from other woodpeckers at mealtime, when nesting time comes

217

it does exactly what the rest of its relatives do; it uses a hollow in a tree or post.

The father and mother flickers make the hollow with their bills. They seem to like this sort of carpenter work, for they often make several holes and then choose the best one for their nest.

Flickers sometimes live in the woods far from cities; but they do not mind being near people if the people do not disturb them, and very often they are found in city parks. There are flickers living even in the great city of New York. They carve their nesting holes in trees that have rather soft places in them or in poles or other wooden places.

Everybody who really knows a flicker likes him for his queer and interesting ways and for his beauty. His coat is mostly gray, with black bars on the outside, but the wings are lined underneath with golden yellow. On the back of his neck he wears a scarlet band, and on his breast he has a black crescent.

The flicker is an early riser and is often awake by four o'clock in the morning. He loves to welcome the day with a racket, the kind he can make by drumming with his bill. So if you hear a loud tapping outside your window early some morning, it may be that a flicker is there drumming his daylight tune, and I hope that you will not be too sleepy to enjoy it.

A Beaver's House

There was a time when there were more beavers than men along the streams of the wooded parts of North America. If there were as many now as then, you would have seen a beaver house yourself and you would have no need to read about one.

Two poplar trees that beavers cut with their teeth.

A three-year-old beaver is about thirty inches tall when it stands on its hind legs. How tall are you? Such a beaver weighs about fifty pounds. Is that more than you weigh or not so much?

The beaver is a big relative of squirrels and mice and rats and rabbits and muskrats and woodchucks. These animals (and some others) are called *rodents*. Each kind lives its own sort of life, but there is one thing that all rodents can do. They can all nibble with sharp front teeth. None of them can nibble better than a beaver.

In fact, a beaver can do with his strong front teeth what a man cannot do without a sharp tool. He can cut through the trunk of a tree. He does not do it with one bite; but he slices out chips, one at a time, making some upward cuts and some downward cuts, so that the gnawed part is shaped somewhat like an hour-glass, sloping both ways to a slender middle. When the beaver has taken out chips enough from all sides of the trunk, the tree breaks at the slender part and comes crashing down.

Beavers like to eat bark; and since they cannot climb trees to get it, they chop down the trees. They do not waste any of the bark they work so hard to get. They eat even what is on the chips. They feast on bark all summer, and they store enough under water (some of it on branches and some peeled off) to last all winter. The beavers weight down their harvest of bark so that it cannot float away or be frozen into the ice.

What becomes of all the branches and trunks of the trees that the beavers chop down? Do they go to waste? Not at all. These the beavers cut with their teeth into lengths they can handle; and part of them they use in building dams which keep the water around their houses from getting too low.

Part of the logs and sticks they use in building their houses. These are rounded at the top, being shaped somewhat like the snow houses that Eskimos build. Branches piled criss-cross, with nothing else, would not keep out the cold or make a house strong enough to stand in the water. So the beavers pack their walls thick with mud and water plants. When that freezes and dries it shuts out the cold; it locks out, too, any wild animals that would like to have a dinner of beaver steak.

A beaver building its house.

Inside the house is a tidy, smooth-walled room above water. This is a snug and comfortable living room. There is a cellar under the floor of the living room. This cellar is full of water nearly to the top. There is a hole in the floor of the living room through which the beavers pass when they go down cellar. From the cellar there is a passageway that leads into the water of the pond. When the beavers are hungry in winter, they can swim under the ice and reach their pantry supplies of bark.

Of course an animal that builds dams and houses in the water and cuts down trees must have a special sort of body. You already know that the beaver's front teeth are sharp and strong. His flat, wide, hairless, paddle-shaped tail is a help in swimming. Do you know how else a beaver uses his tail? The soft thick fur next to his body is waterproof. His hind feet are shaped for swimming. His front paws are used as hands in working. His mouth and ears and nostrils are fitted with flaps that can be drawn so as to keep the water out.

These are some of the things about his body that make it possible for a beaver to be an expert builder of dams, some of which are strong enough to last a hundred years and more. As for his house, it is suited to his needs; and this wonderful rodent can be as comfortable in his home as you can be in yours.

Since the beaver always builds his house in the water, he must use trees that grow near wet places. He likes best of all to build with the branches and trunks of poplar trees. He likes to eat poplar bark better than any other kind. So the same sort of tree gives him both food and shelter.

Now you know how to choose a farm for beavers. If you find a place with plenty of water and plenty of poplar trees, that would please these animals very well. Once there were beavers along nearly every good-sized stream and beside nearly every pond in this country where poplar trees grew. Beavers have been killed for their fur, which is beautiful and warm to wear, and for their flesh, which is good to eat. There are now so few of them left that some people think it would be well to have beaver farms for these animals. There is a great deal of land in the northern United States that has been burned over, where poplars have begun to grow. Such a place seems to be waiting for the beavers to come.

How Trees Shelter People

Before people had tools and learned to be carpenters, they could use trees for shelter only in simple ways. They could go under the branches of trees to be away from the rain or the heat of the sun. They could make some use of such wood as they could get without tools.

We still use trees to protect us from weather. We seek the shade of growing trees, and carpenters build us houses of wood.

Trees with Broad Leaves

When white people came to this country from England, they loved the American elms they found here, because they reminded them of the elms they had loved in England. So they planted elm trees near their homes. People in New England have done this ever since, and there are now many of these large graceful trees in door-yards where they shade houses in summer. Sometimes these trees have been planted, too, on both sides of the village streets, and their branches touch like high arches overhead, giving a pleasant shade.

You do not need to be in New England, however, to see American elms, for these trees grow in most parts of

An elm tree is beautiful even in winter, when it has no leaves.

America east of the Rocky Mountains. They grow in lovely shapes that look somewhat like vases and plumes, and so people sometimes call them *vase elms* and *plume elms*.

The wood from elms is strong and hard to split. It is used in making cars and wagons and boats and floors and furniture and handles for tools.

Another tree that grows in many places in this country is the *paper birch* or *canoe birch* (also called *white birch*). The bark of this tree is white on the outside and yellow inside, and can be split into thin, paper-like layers.

As the bark of this tree is waterproof, it can be used for many things. The Indians made canoes of it, and pails for catching maple sap. Even in wet weather it is good for kindling fires. Indians used to tear the bark into strips and tie them into bundles and use them for torches. People sometimes cut pieces of bark from a tree of this sort while it is still growing. If the bark around the trunk is cut through to the wood underneath and taken off, the tree will die.

224

The canoe birch is a very beautiful tree, and there are other kinds of beautiful birch trees with different kinds of bark.

The wood of birch trees is used for floors and furniture and for many other purposes.

People in many countries have long loved *oak* trees. Many, many years ago some people thought that certain oaks could speak, and that it was

A group of birch trees.

wicked to cut them down. Even now, in some places in England, it is thought that it brings bad luck to cut down an oak tree.

There have been many famous oak trees in England. One was called the Royal Oak because once a king hid from his enemies among its branches. Because the king escaped, English children had a holiday, called "oak apple day," every year in May. The boys cut branches that could be spared from the oak trees. The girls gathered

"People in many countries have long loved oak trees."

blossoms to put with the oak leaves to make the village pretty. They played merry games on oak apple day.

Do you know what an *oak apple* is? You do not need to go to England to see one. Very likely there may be one on the first oak you see. An oak apple is a round growth that is often found on an oak leaf. It is caused by a very tiny insect that puts her egg in the young leaf. Then, as the leaf grows, a big round green "apple" on it grows, too. In the middle of the round "apple" is the baby of the tiny insect. When it is grown and has wings, it bites a hole in the oak apple (which is brown by this time) and flies away.

An oak apple is a kind of plant *gall*. Many kinds of insects change the shapes of growing stems or leaves. Such stems or leaves have enlarged parts or swellings on them. These parts with queer shapes are called galls. The galls are the homes of young gall-insects that live there until they are ready to fly.

The insect that lives in an oak apple has four wings when it is grown. It is shaped much like a tiny wasp. One kind of gall that grows on willows is shaped like a cone. The insect that grows in such a gall has two wings and looks much like a mosquito. Some queer-shaped galls on elm leaves are caused by certain aphids. Some moths make galls.

Oak trees do not have real apples, as you know. Their seeds are nuts, called *acorns*. All kinds of oaks have acorns, though some grow to be twenty years old before there are acorns on them.

There are many kinds of oaks. The *white oak* and its nearest relatives have leaves with rounded scallops (or with no scallops at all). These oaks have acorns that ripen in one summer, and so there are no half-grown acorns on their branches in winter. The nuts of white oaks are sweet, and people as well as many wild animals like them to eat.

The *black oak* and its nearest relatives have leaves with pointed scallops. It takes two summers to ripen their nuts, and so there are half-grown acorns on their twigs in winter. The acorns of these trees are bitter, but the Indians used to soak them in something that took away the bitter taste and made them good to eat.

In the days before steel and iron were used in ships, shipbuilders liked to use oak because this wood is strong and lasts longer under water than most other kinds. Some houses that have been built of oak wood have lasted for hundreds of years. Oak is used for doors and floors and furniture and for other purposes.

Elm, birch, oak, and many other trees are called *broadleaf trees* because their leaves are broad and flat and different from the slender, needle-shaped leaves of pines and other trees that have cones.

In the North, where there is much snow in winter, most trees with broad leaves drop their leaves in autumn. That is why this season is called *fall*, because the leaves fall then.

Do you know what would happen to the broadleaf trees if their leaves were not shed before winter? One year in Maine a heavy snowstorm came on the twelfth of October. The leaves were still on the trees. Some were green and some were yellow and some were red. The snow on these leaves was a beautiful sight. But so much snow piled on them that the trees could not stand the weight. Some of the birch trees bent until their tips touched the ground. The tops of many maple trees were broken off. Oaks were badly damaged. The trunks of some great elms split in pieces from their branches to the ground. The morning after the storm, the air was full of the groaning, cracking sounds of breaking trees. People needed to keep away from trees to be safe from falling branches.

"Some of the birch trees bent until their tips touched the ground."

No one who saw that October snowstorm can doubt that it is well for the broadleaf trees that snow does not often come until their leaves have dropped. Their bare branches are able to stand most winter storms.

Trees with Cones

The only trees that were not harmed by that snowstorm of October twelfth were the pines and their relatives. They, too, were loaded with snow, but their leaves and branches could stand it.

These tall trees are cone-bearing evergreens in the far North. See how straight they stand. Notice the dog team and the sled.

People who live in the North like to see the evergreen leaves of the cone-bearing trees. When the ground is white with snow and other trees are bare, the green color of the pines and their cousins (*spruce* and *cedar* and *fir* and *hemlock*) is welcome to the eye.

230

People are not alone in making use of pine trees.
This long-horned beetle grew up inside a pine tree,
in a tunnel about as large around as a pencil.

Do you know what state is called the "Pine Tree State"? Pines are not all in any one state. Indeed, pines of one kind or another are to be found throughout the length and breadth of our country.

It is because the pines and their relatives are lovely in winter that people choose them for Christmas trees and load them with gay and glittering things that never grow on their branches.

There is something that does grow on these branches that squirrels would rather have than Christmas presents. The cones of some spruce trees that I see each winter are gathered by squirrels and heaped in piles on the ground. The squirrels have little paths leading from the trunk of some tree to these near-by piles and can find them even after the snow has covered them. They do not eat the cones, but they like the seeds that are in them.

All the relatives of the pines have their seeds in cones, and these trees are called *conifers*.

There are many uses for the wood of conifers. Much of the lumber that is sawed from their straight trunks is used in building. Many of us owe our shelter from summer sun and winter storm to the cone-bearing trees.

The carpenter can build a house
　　With floors of birch or other wood,
And beams of oak and walls of pine—
　　A shelter that is warm and good.

But carpenters cannot make trees
　　Or floors such as the forests know
Or halls like pathways through the woods,
　　For things like these must grow.

I like the shelter of a house,
　　But better, far, I love the trees
With trunks that stand against the wind
　　And leaves that whisper in the breeze.

Feeding young robins.

233

CHAPTER XV

QUESTIONS AND EXERCISES

After You Have Read Chapter I

Questions To Answer

1. Of what use is sugar to plants?

2. Name three plants from which men take sugar. Where is the sugar stored in each? Which of these plants were brought to America from some other country?

3. What is nectar? What is pollen? What do bees do with each?

4. How do honeybees look before they are old enough to have wings? What do they eat when they are young?

5. What is honeydew? What are aphids?

Something To Do Outdoors and Indoors

1. See if a boy or girl in your class can bring to school one or more of these things: a maple leaf, a beet root, a piece of sugar cane, a piece of sorgo stalk.

2. Find out what kind of sugar or syrup your mother uses in cooking.

3. Make a list of five facts about honeybees that you think are interesting.

4. Find some honeydew. A good way to look for it is to watch ants running over leaves or up stems until you see where they go. Tell what color the aphids are that the ants visit, and something about their shape. Watch the ants "milk their cows." Do the ants harm the aphids in any way?

5. See whether some of the aphids have wings or whether they are all wingless. Hunt for some that have wing pads (four little flaps on their bodies where wings will come). Place some of the largest of these carefully on leaves in a covered glass. See when they shed their skins and have wings.

6. Watch some flowers and see if bees visit them for nectar or pollen. Notice which they gather. See whether other kinds of insects, besides bees, come to the flowers for nectar or pollen.

AFTER YOU HAVE READ CHAPTER II

Questions To Answer

1. By what name do we call all those animals that feed milk to their young? Name one such animal that flies. Name one (or more) that can swim.

2. Why is milk an important food?

3. What kind of animal gives most of the milk that

is used by people living in the United States? What two other kinds are kept by people in some countries for the sake of their milk?

4. From what are these foods made: curd, cheese, butter, ice cream?

5. What do we mean when we say that an animal hibernates? What do we mean by a *quadruped*?

6. In what ways are cows and deer alike?

Something To Do Outdoors and Indoors

1. Make a list of as many of the mammals mentioned in Chapter II as you can remember. Place a cross after the names of those you have seen.

2. Choose two of the mammals in your list and write five facts about each of the two.

3. If you can visit a farm or a zoo or a circus or a museum, see how many mammals you can find.

4. Look at the feet of a horse (or a zebra) and of a cow (or a deer). How do they differ?

5. Watch the dooryard in the early evening and see if there are bats flying overhead.

AFTER YOU HAVE READ CHAPTER III

Questions To Answer

1. What is a seed? In what part of a plant does it grow? Of what use are seeds to plants?

2. What are five ways in which seeds may travel? Name one kind that travels in each way.

3. How can you start a new plant of certain kinds even if you do not have seeds? What are some of the plants that can be started without seeds?

4. If you have not already done so, answer the questions in the first part of Chapter III.

Something To Do Outdoors and Indoors

1. Hunt for seeds. If you find them on the plants, see how they are growing. If you find them on the ground, see if you can tell whether they are near the parent plant.

2. See if you can find seeds that travel in the different ways you learned about in Chapter III.

3. Plant a few different kinds of seeds, a bulb, a tuber, and a slip in some earth in the schoolroom and take care of them.

4. Find out about some of the seeds (either whole or crushed or ground) that your mother uses for breakfast food, in making bread, or in other food. Ask to see if there are any seeds in her spice box.

5. Find other plants besides dandelions that spread their lower leaves on the ground and thus keep other plants from coming too near.

6. If you can find a milkweed, hunt for striped caterpillars feeding on it. This is a good kind of caterpillar for you to take care of at home or in the schoolroom.

You can keep one in a covered glass jar. There will be air enough in the jar for the caterpillar and the leaves will keep fresher if the jar is covered. Wash and wipe the inside of the jar and put in fresh leaves every day. When the caterpillar stops eating leaves, give it a stick or a box to climb over. Watch it spin. It will not make a cocoon but it will do something else just as interesting. See what happens to it.

7. See if you can find a wild sunflower in blossom. Dig up some of its tubers and see what they are like.

AFTER YOU HAVE READ CHAPTER IV

Questions To Answer

1. What interests you most about a centipede?

2. What is a *decapod?* How does a mother crayfish care for her eggs?

3. What is a *hexapod?* Name three hexapods and tell something about each.

4. What does an animal with a skeleton on the outside of its body do when it grows larger?

5. How do yellow-jacket hornets build a nest?

Something To Do Outdoors and Indoors

1. If you live near water where your parents permit you to go, hunt for crabs or crayfish and tell your teacher what you see them do.

2. Watch a spider while it is hunting.

3. Make a list of the six-footed animals spoken of in Chapter IV. Put a cross after the names of those you have seen.

4. Try to find some insects not spoken of in Chapter IV. Keep some that you can feed and make comfortable for a few days and watch to see what things they do.

5. If you live where there are dragon flies, watch some while they hunt, while they lay their eggs. Try to find a sleeping dragon fly.

6. Hunt for a hornets' nest in winter when it is empty and find how it looks inside.

After You Have Read Chapter V

Questions To Answer

1. If sometime you have a chance to go hunting with a camera, of what animal would you like best to take a picture? What do you think is most interesting about the animal you choose?

2. What are some of the animals that help keep the earth and water clean? Which ones have you seen?

3. How do some birds help farmers by hunting?

4. Have you ever seen a snake? What are some of the things snakes do?

5. How are fish different from whales?

Something To Do Outdoors and Indoors

1. Make a list of five questions about the animals in this chapter for your classmates to answer.

2. Try to find a fish to watch. If you live near a brook or other water where you are permitted to go, look there. See if someone can bring a fish in a fish bowl to school for a few days.

3. If you know a cat, tell some of the things you have seen it do.

4. If you know a dog, tell what you like best about it.

AFTER YOU HAVE READ CHAPTER VI

Questions To Answer

1. Which plant belonging to the Mallow Family is of most importance to people? What are four or more uses of this plant?

2. In which parts of the United States does this plant grow? Why do people not have it in all the states?

3. About how big does this plant grow? What sort of flowers and seeds does it have?

4. How are its seeds picked and what do people do with them?

Something To Do Outdoors and Indoors

1. Hunt for one or more of the plants belonging to the Mallow Family, spoken of in this chapter. If you can, bring samples to school.

2. Look through a window of a dry-goods store and see what things you think are made of cotton.

3. Make a list of the things to eat that grow on plants of the Mallow Family, spoken of in this chapter. Make a cross after the names of those you have eaten.

AFTER YOU HAVE READ CHAPTER VII

Questions To Answer

1. What is meant by a plant *fiber?* What use do some birds make of fibers?

2. Name five plants whose fibers are used by people and tell how they are used.

3. What does the word *boll* mean? Name two plants that have bolls.

4. What is meant by *Irish linen?*

5. What did people who lived long ago in Egypt do with linen? How do we know?

Something To Do Outdoors and Indoors

1. Hunt for plants with fibers. See if you can tie knots in them without breaking them. See if you can

braid them. Do such fibers break more easily when they are wet or when they are dry?

2. Read about "A Flax Game" on pages 122–123 of this book. Do at school as many of the things as your teacher will permit.

After You Have Read Chapter VIII

Questions To Answer

1. What is silk? In what ways is a fiber of silk different from a cotton fiber or a flax fiber or other plant fiber?

2. What are some of the differences in the following stages of an insect: *egg, caterpillar, pupa, moth?* Which stage seems most interesting to you? Why?

Something To Do Outdoors and Indoors

1. Find spider webs of different shapes and sizes. See whether the spiders in them are all the same size, shape, and color. Watch a spider spin. Notice where the silk comes out of a spider's body. Watch to see how a spider fastens the silk in making a web.

2. Find caterpillars of different sorts and watch them spin. Notice where the silk comes out of a caterpillar's body.

3. Hunt for caterpillars doing one or more of these things: spinning a molting mat on which to rest while it sheds its skin; dropping down from a leaf by its "life line"; making a tent of silk in the angle of branches in

the spring; making a silk nest which covers the tips of large branches in summer; making a small nest in the fall in which to spend the winter; spinning a cocoon.

4. Keep some caterpillars at school until they spin some silk. If they are hungry and growing, feed them leaves of the same kind as those on which you found them.

5. Write five questions about silkworms for your classmates to answer.

6. Take a piece of spider silk or caterpillar silk and see if you can tie knots in it or braid it without breaking the fiber.

7. Soak an empty cocoon, from which the moth has escaped, in hot water and see if you can separate the fibers and wind them on a spool.

AFTER YOU HAVE READ CHAPTER IX

Questions To Answer

1. What is a *mammal?* Are all the animals mentioned in Chapter IX mammals?

2. What is a *quadruped?* Are all the animals mentioned in Chapter IX quadrupeds?

3. Answer the questions on pages 153–154.

Something To Do Outdoors and Indoors

1. Make a list of all the animals you can think of

that have fur coats. Put a cross after the names of those you have seen.

2. Try to see some fur animals on a farm or at a circus or in a zoo. Visit, if you can, a museum and ask to see fur animals.

3. Look through some books for pictures of fur animals that are not in this book.

4. Which of the fur animals you have looked at have bodies most like the following: cat, dog, cow, rat? Tell in what ways.

5. Write what you think would be five good laws to help protect wild animals.

AFTER YOU HAVE READ CHAPTER X

Questions To Answer

1. How do people living in the northern part of the United States keep their hens comfortable in winter? Do geese and ducks and turkeys need protection from cold winter storms?

2. What are some of the habits of the following birds: bluebird, robin, swallow, hummingbird? What colors are each? Where does each stay in winter?

3. Do robins and sparrows take baths in deep or shallow water? Do they swim?

4. Is there a Junior Audubon Club at your school?

Something To Do Outdoors and Indoors

1. Look at the picture of the bird on page 54 of this book. It is a thrush. Note its spotted breast. What two birds of the Thrush Family are spoken of in Chapter X? Do they have spotted breasts? What is the thrush on page 54 eating? Find out whether other birds of the Thrush Family like fruit to eat. Watch a robin or a bluebird. What does it eat? Where does it build its nest? What does it catch to feed its young? Find out whether all birds of the Thrush Family eat insects.

2. If you live where there is snow in winter, watch for two birds that eat weed seeds in winter. Watch for two that hunt for insects or insect eggs hidden on branches or in cracks about the trunks of trees. Find out what you can do to help keep the seed-eaters and the insect-eaters plump and happy during the cold weather. Find out which of the winter birds will eat suet and unsalted nuts (never feed salty things to birds). Find out which ones will eat crumbs and seeds which you can give them. While you are watching birds out of doors you will, of course, be very careful to have good manners. At such times people try to keep their voices low and gentle, and their movements slow. It is not kind to go near enough a bird to frighten it.

3. Listen to birds when they are singing and try to learn how to tell some of them by their songs. Listen when they are calling to each other and try to see if you

can make sounds enough like their calls so that they will answer you.

4. If you live in a city, find out where you can find wild birds to watch.

5. Write five questions about English sparrows and five about pigeons for your classmates to answer.

6. Find out how to answer the questions about feathers on page 166 of this book.

After You Have Read Chapter XI

Questions To Answer

1. How can an earthworm sense the difference between light and darkness? In what way is it warned when you come near its hole? How can it breathe without lungs or gills? How does it make a hole in which to live?

2. Where does a queen bumblebee stay in the fall of the year? In the winter? What does she do in the spring? In the summer?

3. Why is one kind of turtle called a painted turtle? What part of its life does a painted turtle spend in a hole in the ground?

4. In what ways are the habits of bank swallows different from those of tree swallows?

5. If you find a cricket, how can you tell whether it is laying eggs?

6. What would you best like to see a woodchuck do?

Something To Do Outdoors and Indoors

1. Hunt for holes in the ground in which insects or spiders live. Watch them come and go. Tell what you see them do.

2. Find a place where you can dig with a spade or a trowel. If you find any little creatures living in the dirt, notice how they look and how they move.

3. Fill a flowerpot with earth and put in some earthworms. Put on top of the earth some bits of food you think the worms will like. Count the bits and see if any of them are gone the next morning. Soak a few old brown fallen leaves and place them in the flowerpot. Look in the morning to see if the worms have moved them during the night.

4. Make a list of as many animals as you know about, besides those mentioned in this chapter, that live or hide things in caves or holes in the ground. Put a cross after those you have seen.

AFTER YOU HAVE READ CHAPTER XII

Questions To Answer

1. In what ways are eave swallows different from tree swallows and bank swallows?

2. In what ways are mason wasps different from the kinds of wasps that live in paper nests (hornets)?

3. What insects, besides a caddis, have you read

about that live in the water while they are too young to have wings?

Something To Do Outdoors and Indoors

1. Make with clay or putty a little jug shaped like that of a mason wasp. Make a nest shaped like that of an eave swallow.

2. If you live near a stream or pond that your parents permit you to visit, hunt for caddis cases. See if you can find some like those in the picture on page 188 of this book. See if you can find some other kinds. Watch to see how a caddis inside its case moves about. Look at the winged insects that are on stems near the edge of the water and see if there are any that you think may be grownup caddis flies.

3. Some warm evening see how many kinds of insects will come into the open window of a lighted room. Or, if there is a screen in the window, see how many kinds will come to the outside of the screen.

4. Watch to see if insects are flying about an electric street light in the evening.

5. Try to get a firefly to look at. If you find a beetle in the daytime that you think may be a firefly, take it into a dark closet and find out whether part of its body gives off light.

After You Have Read Chapter XIII

Questions To Answer

1. If you have ever seen a snail, tell what you saw it do. If you have never seen a snail, tell what things you would best like to see one do.

2. What is a *leaf miner?* Does the little caterpillar on the apple leaf live in a "mine" before or after it lives in a "case"?

3. How do the little case bearers on apple and larch trees differ from the one on sweet fern?

Something To Do Outdoors and Indoors

1. Hunt for leaves in which leaf miners are living, or have been living. You can know such a leaf by the brown place where the green part has been eaten out. Find different kinds of leaves that have been mined. Notice that the mines are different shapes.

2. Make drawings to show the shapes of the leaves and the shapes of the mines. Find out the names of the plants from which you pick mined leaves.

3. Hunt for case bearers on different kinds of plants. Keep some which you can easily supply with fresh food every day. When they are through eating, put them in a box and look often to see when the full-grown insects with wings come out of the cases.

AFTER YOU HAVE READ CHAPTER XIV

Questions To Answer

1. In what ways are tree frogs like some other frogs? In what ways are they different?

2. In what ways are tree frogs like toads? In what ways are they different?

3. How can you know whether a leaf-cutter bee has been visiting a rosebush?

4. What is the favorite food of a flicker? Where do other woodpeckers find most of their food?

5. What other animal that you have read about makes a winter house in water shaped somewhat like that of a beaver?

6. How can you tell a broadleaf tree from a cone-bearing tree in summer? In winter?

7. What is an *evergreen* tree? Can you name one cone-bearing tree that is not an evergreen? Can you name one broadleaf tree that is an evergreen?

Something To Do Outdoors and Indoors

1. If you live where there is snow in winter, notice on what parts of a cone-bearing tree there is most snow. Is it near the tips of the branches or near the trunk of the tree? Can you tell, from the shape of the tree, why?

2. On what parts of an elm, oak, or maple is there

most snow? Can you tell, from the shape of the tree, why?

3. Make a list of as many animals as you can think of that live in holes in trees or in homes made of wood. Place a cross after the names of those you have seen.

4. Make a clay house to show how you think a beaver's house is shaped.

5. Choose a favorite broadleaf tree that you can watch. Find out its name. Notice when it blossoms and what colors its flowers are. Watch for the seeds and gather some. Plant some and find out how a very young tree looks. Look at the twigs of the tree in winter. Can you find buds of next spring's leaves? What color are the leaves of your tree in the fall? What is meant by the *fall* of the year?

6. Choose a favorite cone-bearing tree. Find out whether it ever sheds its leaves. Are there any of its old leaves on the ground under the branches? Bring in some full-grown cones before they have dropped their seeds and keep them at home or in the schoolroom until they open. See during the winter if you can find seeds of the same sort on the snow. See what sort of tracks there are near the seeds. Try to find out what animals make these tracks when they come to eat the seeds.

7. Hunt for galls on spruce trees. Try to find one that is shaped somewhat like a little pineapple. Hunt for galls on oak and elm and willow and other broadleaf trees. Make drawings to show the shapes of the different galls you find.

CPSIA information can be obtained
at www.ICGtesting.com
Printed in the USA
BVHW081556100719
553091BV00001B/84/P

9 781633 340992